2

THE BROSS LIBRARY

VOLUME II

THE BROSS LECTURES · · 1904

THE BIBLE

ITS ORIGIN AND NATURE

SEVEN LECTURES DELIVERED BEFORE
LAKE FOREST COLLEGE
ON THE FOUNDATION OF THE LATE
WILLIAM BROSS

BY THE REVEREND

MARCUS DODS, D.D.

PROFESSOR OF EXEGETICAL THEOLOGY
IN NEW COLLEGE, EDINBURGH

Association Press

NEW YORK: 124 EAST 28TH STREET
LONDON: 47 PATERNOSTER ROW, E. C.
1912

THESE LECTURES

Are Gratefully Dedicated

TO

THE PRESIDENT AND PROFESSORS OF

LAKE FOREST COLLEGE

AND TO THE OTHER FRIENDS THERE
WHOSE HOSPITALITY AND KINDLINESS
MADE THEIR DELIVERY
AN UNUSUAL PLEASURE
AND A LASTING MEMORY
TO
THE AUTHOR

THE BROSS FOUNDATION

In 1879, the late William Bross of Chicago, lieutenant-governor of Illinois in 1866–70, desiring to make some memorial of his son, Nathaniel Bross, who had died in 1856, entered into an agreement with the "Trustees of Lake Forest University," whereby there was finally transferred to the said Trustees the sum of forty thousand dollars, the income of which was to accumulate in perpetuity for successive periods of ten years, at compound interest, the accumulations of one decade to be spent in the following decade, for the purpose of stimulating the production of the best books or treatises "*on the connection, relation, and mutual bearing of any practical science, or the history of our race, or the facts in any department of knowledge, with and upon the Christian Religion.*"

In his deed of gift the founder had in view "*the religion of the Bible, composed of the Old and New Testaments of our Lord and Saviour, Jesus Christ, as commonly received in the Presbyterian and other evangelical churches.*" His object was "*to call out the best efforts of the highest talent and the ripest scholarship of the world, to*

vii

illustrate from science, or any department of knowledge, and to demonstrate, the divine origin and authority of the Christian Scriptures; and, further, to show how both Science and Revelation coincide, and to prove the existence, the providence, or any or all of the attributes of the one living and true God, infinite, eternal, and unchangeable in His being, wisdom, power, holiness, justice, goodness, and truth."

At the close of the Trust Agreement, the donor expressed the hope that, by means of this fund, the various authors might, "*every ten years, post up the science of the world and show how it illustrates the truth of the Bible, and the existence of God,*" and that thereby "*the gospel of our blessed Saviour, Jesus Christ, and the glories of His sacrifice and plan of salvation*" might be preached "*to the end of time.*"

The gift thus contemplated in the original agreement of 1879 was finally consummated in 1890. The first decade of the accumulations of interest having closed in 1900, the Trustees of the Bross Fund began at that time the administration of this important trust.

The Trust Agreement prescribed two methods by which the production of books of the above-mentioned character was to be stimulated: —

1. One or more premiums or prizes were to be offered during each decade, the competition

for which was to be thrown open to "the scientific men, the Christian philosophers and historians of all nations."

Accordingly, a prize of six thousand dollars has been offered for the best book fulfilling any of the purposes described in the foregoing extracts from the Trust Agreement, the competing manuscripts to be presented on or before June 1, 1905; for full particulars as to this prize, application should be made to the undersigned.

Once in every fifty (or thirty years, according as the Trustees of the fund may decide at the time) the entire amount of simple interest accumulated during the previous decade is to be offered as a single premium or prize for a similar competition.

2. The Trustees of the Bross Fund were also empowered from time to time to select and appoint particular scholars, who should prepare books, upon some theme within the terms of the Trust Agreement, that would "illustrate" or "demonstrate" or commend the Christian Religion, or *any* phase of it, to the times in which we live.

Ordinarily, it is proposed that the writers of the books thus prepared should be asked to deliver the substance of such books in the form of lectures before Lake Forest College, and any of the general public who may desire to attend them, such courses to be known as the Bross Lectures.

The Trust Agreement further provides for the publication, by the Trustees of the Bross Fund, of the books prepared under either of the two methods above described.

Two writers have already been specially appointed in pursuance of the second method: —

The first was the Reverend President Francis Landey Patton, D.D., LL.D., of the Princeton Theological Seminary, who, in May, 1903, delivered a course of five lectures before Lake Forest College, on "Obligatory Morality." These lectures are now the property of the Trustees of the Bross Fund, and will be published in due season after the author has been given the opportunity to revise and expand them.

The second of the writers thus specially appointed was the Reverend Professor Marcus Dods, D.D., of New College, Edinburgh, who, in May, 1904, delivered a course of lectures before Lake Forest College, on "The Bible: Its Origin and Nature." These lectures are embodied in the present volume.

As a token of the donor's affectionate remembrance of his "friend and teacher," the late Mark Hopkins, the distinguished President of

Williams College, and as recording his own appreciation of the notable work done by President Hopkins in commending the Christian Religion to his own day and generation, the founder of the Bross Fund further directed its trustees to acquire the book written by Dr. Hopkins on "The Evidences of Christianity," and to publish the same as "Number one of the series of books to be prepared under the arrangement" provided for by the Bross Foundation. This book has already been purchased from the executors of President Hopkins' estate, and will be published, at an early date, as Volume I of the Bross Library. Dr. Dods' lectures are being published, therefore, as Volume II.

RICHARD D. HARLAN,

President of Lake Forest College.

LAKE FOREST, ILLINOIS,
CHRISTMAS, 1904.

CONTENTS

I

THE BIBLE AND OTHER SACRED BOOKS

I

THE BIBLE AND OTHER SACRED BOOKS

THE designation by which Muhammad in the Quran usually distinguishes Christians is "the people of the book." This, however, is merely an illustration of the prophet's limited horizon. For, in point of fact, the possession of sacred scriptures was not then and is not now a distinctive peculiarity of Christianity. Religions now extinct, and even in Muhammad's time obsolete, such as the ancient Egyptian and Babylonian, had their sacred writings. So have the great religions which now share with Christianity the adhesion of mankind, — Zoroastrianism, Brahmanism, Buddhism, Confucianism, and Muhammadanism itself.

Sacred writings not peculiar to Christianity.

Singularly enough it was the most literary of ancient races which possessed no sacred writings. Among the Greeks their place was filled by oracular responses, the prognostications of augurs, and omens of various kinds;

No sacred books in Greece or Rome.

while the traditions regarding their gods and
the most authoritative religious and ethical
ideas were transmitted in Homer, Plato, and
the great Tragedians.   In Rome, the place left
vacant by the absence of authoritative scriptures was filled, as the nation became sensible
of religious cravings, by the didactic philosophy
and preaching of the later Stoics. And although
the Greek philosophers and tragedians and the
Roman Stoics laid no claim to inspiration or
final authority, they yet wrote on an extraordi-
narily high level of feeling and of thought, and
they gave utterance to much that has entered
into and become a permanent element in the
religious life of modern Europe.   Teachings of
the deepest kind regarding the moral order of
the world and the relation of man to things
unseen abound in their writings, which are still
read with admiration and with profit.   Yet
those remarkable utterances cannot be classed
as sacred books.

*Sacred
books of the
East.*
The great Eastern religions, however, are
rich in sacred scriptures.   Until a few years
ago all these, with the exception of the Quran,
were locked up in little-known languages, —
Zend, Sanskrit, Cingalese, Chinese.   Recently,
however, they have been rapidly made accessible to the English-reading public, especially in

the great series of " The Sacred Books of the
East," initiated and edited by the late Professor
Max Müller, and already numbering about fifty
volumes.

It has become the fashion in certain quarters *Character*
to magnify these books and to leave it to be *of these*
inferred that there is little to choose between *books.*
them and our Bible. It might be enough in
correction of this phase of religious dilettantism
to cite the words of Max Müller's editorial
preface to the series : " I confess," he says, " it
has been for many years a problem to me, aye,
and to a great extent is so still, how the Sacred
Books of the East should, by the side of so
much that is fresh, natural, simple, beautiful,
and true, contain so much that is not only un-
meaning, artificial, and silly, but even hideous
and repellent."   Elsewhere he says of the
Brahmanas: " These works deserve to be
studied as the physician studies the twaddle of
idiots and the ravings of madmen.   They will
disclose to a thoughtful eye the ruins of faded
grandeur ; the memories of noble aspirations.
But let us only try to translate these works
into our own language, and we shall feel aston-
ished that human language and human thought
should ever have been used for such purposes."

It would indeed be difficult to name any

books which more seriously try the patience of
the reader. We may doggedly plough through
them to gain some insight into the state of
mind of those who once found or still find in
them their highest teaching, but no one who
has been brought up in Christian ideas and
modern thought need expect to find in them
religious stimulus or useful knowledge. At
the same time it is not to be denied, but rather
thankfully acknowledged, that in some of them
ethical teaching of a very high and pure strain
is to be found. Singularly enough this is
Confucian especially true of the Confucian and Buddhist
and Bud- books, which can only by courtesy be called
dhist Ethics. *sacred* books. For Confucius was a professed
agnostic. " To give one's self earnestly to the
duties due to man, and while respecting spiritual beings, to keep aloof from them " — this, in
his own words, describes his normal attitude.
He would never commit himself either to belief
or disbelief of the spiritual world. He merely
declined to concern himself about matters which
were not of earth. His was a dry, prosaic,
practical mind. He was the typical Chinaman.
But if the Confucian books give us little religion, they promulgate a singularly pure morality. When one of his pupils, weary of maxims
and rules, said to Confucius, " Is there not one

word which may serve as a rule of practice for the whole of life ? " the great teacher replied, " Is not Reciprocity such a word ? What you don't want done to yourself do not to others." This was not a mere accidental hit or happy thought. It was this same idea which pervaded his teaching, and which he again formulated in the ever-memorable expression, as striking as any ethical truth uttered by Western philosophy, " Benevolence is Man." This doctrine of his was taken up by a contemporary philosopher, Mih-Teih, who demonstrated in an elaborate ethical treatise that universal mutual love is the root of all virtue and the cure of all social evil.

In the Buddhist scriptures also there is much ethical teaching of great value. The superiority of purity and love to all ceremonial observances has never been more explicitly or forcibly proclaimed. Never has the eradication of self-will, self-assertion, self-pleasing, been more stringently demanded. " Let a man overcome evil by good ; let him overcome the greedy by liberality, the liar by truth. For hatred does not cease by hatred at any time ; hatred ceases by love." Views and principles of life calculated to make a lasting impression, a code of morals sufficient to guide men to

Buddhist eradication of self-will.

righteousness, might easily be gathered from the Buddhist scriptures. Yet Buddhism has only to a very small extent cleansed society.

Failure of Buddhism.   The failure of Buddhism is probably due to its agnostic attitude toward God and its disbelief in a future life. It is a system of despair, and of despair because of its materialism. Buddha started with a deep impression of the emptiness, sadness, and corruption of human life. The sole escape he saw was to detach one's self to the utmost from life. He was the father of the Stoic and the Monk. To subdue all desire was to become superior to life ; and perfected triumph was to enter Nirvana, a state of passionless, apathetic, unmoved existence or non-existence. This was a view of life he could not possibly have taken had he believed in God, and his system fails because deeper even than the thirst for righteousness is the thirst for God. Without God, and the hope which union with God begets, morality apparently cannot maintain itself among men. This is the lesson which Buddhism writes in legible characters across human history.

Christianity more than Ethics.   If we have believed that the chief distinction between the Bible and other sacred books lies in the contents of their moral teaching, our faith may receive a shock when we find how much of what is true and high those books contain. Hence the reluctance of some to admit the facts. Instead of rejoicing to learn that more of our fellow-men than we had supposed have striven after purity and righteousness, we are actually disappointed and disconcerted. Mr. Kinglake, in his stirring history, our English "Iliad," has admirably shown that the unusual bloodshed at the battle of Inkerman was in great measure due to the false issue on which for part of the day the battle was fought. The Sand Bag Battery, for the possession of which hundreds of brave men fell, was utterly worthless when won, and was not the key of the position ; and yet it was round it that hour after hour the main tide of battle was drawn. Similarly it is only through a complete, and in many cases disastrous misapprehension that the contest between the Bible and rival books can be drawn to a position of second-rate importance. That men should be able to analyze their own moral nature seems as likely as that they should be able to anatomize the human body and discover the purpose and uses and treatment of its organs. At all events, it is a mistake to treat Christianity or the Bible as if it were mainly a system of morals, and to lay the stress of the argument in its favor on its distinct superiority in moral teaching ; because, even though this position be gained, we do not thereby command the whole field. What we seek in our religion, and what those admirable moral teachers wholly fail to give us, is the knowledge of God and the establishment of right relations with Him. ‖ It is this which gives us at once a moral criterion and a moral dynamic. ‖ And it is here the superiority of the Bible appears. We find there the proclamation of God's Fatherhood and the restoration of right relations at once with Him and with our fellow-men.

Non-Christian sacred books not enlightening.

Passing from the merely ethical sacred books to those which profess to accomplish this very thing and restore right relations with God, it must be owned that they are intensely disappointing. Without entering into detail, it may be said generally that these books had the misfortune to be written while religion was in its legal and ceremonial stage. The kind of religion which they represent is rudimentary and has been outgrown by those races which, mainly through the enlightening power of Christianity, have come to believe only in a religion which is inward and spiritual. It is this chiefly which makes these books dead to us and the heaviest of reading. Ceremonial, often of a revolting kind ; magic, the efficacy of repeating certain forms of words, meet us at every step.

Better things might have been expected of the Quran, written as it was nearly six centuries after the New Testament. But the Quran is a dull book. Unlike the other sacred books, it is all the work of one man, and of a man whose genius for religion was concentrated on one point. Like our own Bishop Butler, he believed that the whole of religion was comprised in submission to the Divine will, and that which gave him importance was the extraordinary energy with which he propagated the idea of one sovereign Ruler. With rare exception the Suras of the Quran are characterized rather by force than by felicity of expression : "Verily, those who disbelieve in our signs we will broil them with fire ; whenever their skins are well done, then we will change them for other skins, that they may taste the torment." In the later deliverances it is painfully apparent that Muhammad invented supposed revelations to suit his own convenience and minister to his own pleasures.

The Quran

But its radical or capital condemnation is that it propounds an intensely legal religion. It tells men their duty and enforces it by threats and promises. It finds a sphere among primi-

Radical vice of the Quran.

tive peoples and is accepted as God's word by
over a hundred millions of our race.   But like
police regulations, it is effective only within a
certain circumference, and commits the radical
error of proposing to rectify the conduct, not
the character.   That religion which makes no
provision for transforming *ourselves* and imparting to us a spirit which will express itself in
righteousness is not the ultimate religion.   In
a word, Muhammadanism is two thousand years
out of date.   Whatever help it may furnish to
men at a certain stage of civilization, it can furnish none to any one who understands Christianity.

Nature of
the Bible.

The essential differences between the Bible
and other sacred books will best be understood
by a consideration of the actual nature of the
former ; and to this we now proceed.

Is a written
canon legiti-
mate in
Christian-
ity ?

But no sooner do we set our Bible before us
as an object of inquiry than certain preliminary
questions arise.   These cannot be fully examined now, but one or two of them may at
any rate be alluded to.   First, it may be questioned whether a sacred and authoritative
written canon is a legitimate or necessary ac-
companiment of a purely spiritual religion.   A
written covenant was of the very essence of the
Old Testament dispensation, but no provision

was expressly made by the mediator of the New Covenant for engrossing its terms in a docunent. It may be alleged that it is incongruous that a spiritual religion should be subjected to an outward written rule. The Society of Friends maintains that because the Scriptures "are only a declaration of the Fountain, and not the Fountain itself, therefore they are not to be esteemed the principal ground of all truth and knowledge, nor yet the adequate primary rule of faith and manners." That is to say, the Scriptures are a secondary rule, subordinate to the Spirit. The Church of Rome, too, assigns a first place to the Spirit speaking through Christ's Vicar on earth. Both the Society of Friends and the Church of Rome respond to the claim made by the Christian heart that the Church and the individual should enjoy the guidance of the living Lord and should not be referred back to the first century for all its light and inspiration. And unquestionably if the Bible tends to stifle this cry for a *living* God and prompts us to lean more on the written letter than on the present and active personality of Christ's Spirit, it does harm.

But there is really no incompatibility between the written word and the living Spirit. The figure of Christ is once for all presented in the

No incompatibility between Bible and Spirit.

Gospels, and in the Epistles the relation of the soul to Him is once for all in essentials declared; and these are the means used by the Spirit for bringing men into true fellowship with Christ and filling them with the light which accompanies faithful knowledge of Him. The living Spirit of God is ever the Spirit of Christ.

Origin of the Bible.

Again, we no sooner ask ourselves what the Bible is, than we are led to consider its origin. How did those various books come to be written? Putting ourselves back into the days when as yet there was no written record of the past, with what object in view did the earliest writer commence his work? Probably some early prophet, Amos or Hosea, so stirred the hearts of the people that his words were transcribed, though with little idea that they were to ring in the ears of men for nearly three thousand years. Even before the eighth century there may have been records of important events and legendary accounts of remote transactions. The building up of the books which form our Scriptures, their individual histories and separate fortunes, and their eventual collection to form our Canon, form an extremely interesting subject of investigation, but to pursue it here would take us too far aside from the particular line

we desire to follow; and, besides, full information on these points is easily accessible.

Turning, then, to the Bible itself, we are first
of all struck with the fact that it is not one
book but many — thirty-nine in the Old Testament, twenty-seven in the New. The very
name "Bible" indicates this plurality, because
it represents the *Biblia* of ecclesiastical Latin.
This was the transliteration of the Greek τὰ
βιβλία, but it was used not only as a plural
(*Biblia, -orum*) but as a singular (*Biblia, -ae*).
Hence it has passed into English as a singular,[1]
which only exhibits one side of the Bible. The
Greek word τὸ βιβλίον or ἡ βίβλος, a book, was
derived from the material on which it was written after the Clay period had passed away. This
material was the Byblus or Papyrus, an Egyptian reed out of which the first *paper* was made.
At an early date, the expression αἱ βίβλοι or
τὰ βιβλία was used by the Jews to denote the
books by preëminence, the sacred writings. At
first, some explanatory designation was added,
as in 1 Macc. xii. 9, "the holy books" (τὰ
βιβλία τὰ ἄγια). In Dan. ix. 2, we find ἐν ταῖς
βίβλοις used of Jeremiah's writings; and in

The word "Bible."

[1] Nestle has shown (in *Exp. Times*, Sept., 1904) that
Biblia first appears in English catalogues in the thirteenth
century, Becker's earlier example being wrongly dated.

the Prologue to the Wisdom of Sirach there occurs the classification, " the law, the prophets, and the other hereditary books " (τῶν ἄλλων πατρίων βιβλίων). But the first clear use of τὰ βιβλία without qualifying addition to denote the Bible or the Scriptures is found in the Pseudo-Clement (XIV. 2). Subsequently the usage became common, and how clearly the Patristic and Mediæval writers kept in view the plurality of books forming our Bible, may be gathered from their commonly speaking of it as the " Divine Library " (Bibliotheca Divina).

What bond unites the books?

What, then, is the bond which ties these books together? What is the element which forms the common distinction, at once separating them from other books and uniting them in one whole? It is obvious that alongside of the vast differences existing between these books in date, authorship, form, and style, there must be some common element powerful enough to counterbalance and overcome these differences and bring the books together in one solid body. Within this collection we find traditions dimly emerging out of the mists that obscure the earliest prehistoric times; we find histories based on documents which would seem to have long since passed out of existence, genealogies which aim at connecting later generations with the

progenitors of the race, biographies which immortalize their heroes in a form more monu-
mental than brass ; songs of victory and of love,
hymns wrung from souls subjected to every
species of human distress and agony, and psalms
which serve for every age to utter its praise,
and its penitence, and its thirst for the living
God; the sayings of the worldly wise, and the
inspired warnings, denunciations, and encour-
agements of the prophets of God; we have
drama and essay, the simple gospel story, the
earliest annals of the Church, and the letters of
friendship and counsel that passed from the
founders to their churches. Had the purpose
been to present to our view the various literary
forms employed by the Hebrews during the
whole of their history in their own land, a more
miscellaneous collection could not have been
brought together. If you bound into one volume Knox's " History of the Reformation," the
" Olney Hymns," Bunyan's " Pilgrim's Progress," Savonarola's " Sermons," the " Sayings of
Samuel Johnson," Cowper's " Letters," " Hamlet," you would not have a volume more miscellaneous in form than the Bible.

Yet the unity of the whole is unmistakable.
Individuals may feel that this or that part is
incongruous with the rest ; some may object to

*The unity
unmistak-
able.*

the presence of the Song of Songs, some would
eject Ecclesiastes or Second Peter ; but on the
whole the unity of Scripture has been universally
recognized.   Moreover, this unity is obviously
not designed and artificial; it is not even conscious; the writers of the several parts had no
intention to contribute nor any idea that they
were contributing to one whole.   In uttering
their private confessions and their individual
longings the authors of the Psalms had no idea
they were contributing to an immortal liturgy.
When the worn-out artist relieved his feelings
by penning Ecclesiastes it was scarcely a place
in the Canon he expected; and when Paul
seized the opportunity of a casual post to Asia
Minor and sent a letter to some of his churches
there, he certainly did not anticipate that, two
thousand years after, his expressions would be
reckoned infallible.   And yet when these various writings are drawn together, their unity
becomes apparent.   In what does it consist?

Not the en-
tire litera-
ture of a
race.

At first sight one is apt to fancy that the
unity of Scripture arises from the circumstance
that in the Bible we have the entire extant
literature of a race.   But this at once appears to
be a superficial view.   Even the earliest writers
in the collection depend on documents which
were not received into the sacred archives; and

the later writers had as their contemporaries or successors many authors whose works are partly lost and partly extant, but which have been carefully excluded from the Canon. The works of Philo were numerous, were devoted to sacred subjects, were widely read, were rich in devout suggestions and of great influence; yet no one seems to have dreamt of admitting them into the Canon. In like manner the claims of Josephus were entirely neglected. In regard to the New Testament the same holds good. Our Bible, then, was not formed on the commodious principle of embracing all Hebrew literature. The Canon is not a carpet-bag canon. It is an interesting fact, a fact with its own significance, that all the writers represented in our Bible were, with one exception, Jews. But this is not the reason why their writings, when brought together, are found to form one whole.

Again, it might be thought that the element *Not their godly tone.* which these writings possess in common and which brings them together is the devout or godly tone in which they are written. Dissimilar in the subjects treated, the point of view and the tone are the same. Whether we read a hymn, or a narrative of the exploits of some old hero, or the cynical observations of one who from an actor in life has become a spectator and critic, or predictions of political revolutions, or the annals of the early kings of Israel and Judah, we find in all the same reference to God, the same loyalty to Him, the same confident expectation that He will one day judge the world in righteousness. However various the subjects, however remote the dates, however differently conditioned the authorship, there is everywhere the same faith breathing through the writing. The story of creation is told not in a scientific, but in a religious interest; the traditions of the patriarchs are recorded not for the glorification of the Jewish people, but for the glory of God; the annals of the Kingdom are written not as secular history, but as an illustration of the care with which Jehovah has trained His people; the prophets appear on the field of politics not as ambitious demagogues or fanatical alarmists, but as the voice of God disclosing that at each crisis of history there is a Divine Agent as well as human forces. These books are sacred books.

Though this tone readily discernible.

It is interesting to find how universally it is acknowledged that our Bible is characterized by a consciousness of God and a consequent elevation of tone. Testimonies might be produced from Carlyle, Emerson, Ruskin, Ewald,

Coleridge, Sir Walter Scott, and many other unbiassed sources. But one must suffice. No writer of the last century was more unbridled in thought or speech than Heinrich Heine. In the midst of one of his wildest and most humorous outbreaks he suddenly says: "I owe my conversion simply to the reading of a book. A book? Yes, an old, homely-looking book, modest as nature and as natural as it; a book that has a workaday and unassuming look, like the sun that warms us, like the bread that nourishes us, a book that seems to us as familiar and as full of kindly blessing as the old grandmother who reads daily in it with dear trembling lips and with spectacles on her nose. And the book is called quite shortly — the Book — the Bible." And it is necessary to keep in view this self-evidencing character of the Bible — the something about it which awes and sobers the right-minded reader and makes it independent of criticism and sets it in a place apart. If it is true, as so many writers of various dispositions unexpectedly testify, that the Bible has everywhere nourished the best life that has been known on earth; if it be true that it has in point of fact been the spring of the highest aspirations men have cherished and the ripest character they have attained; if in

every generation it has served for the healing
of the nations, lying at the root of all progress,
and insisting upon a finer and purer civilization; if, wherever it comes, it brings with it
courage and solace in danger and in death; if
it has brought heaven nearer to earth, and if it
reveals God as our Father and enables the
hopeless and broken and abandoned to hope
and to believe, — then certainly there must be
that in the book itself irrespective of our
knowledge of its origin which proclaims it to
be God's message to men.

Not all God's word is Scripture. But even this characteristic, important as it
is, can scarcely be that unifying element which
brings these books together in separation from
all other literature.   For many books might be
named which also possess this characteristic and
which have, perhaps, more directly influenced
men for good than the Scriptures themselves.
God speaks to us through other channels than
Scripture.   In nature, in history, in providence,
in conscience, His voice is heard.   Day by day
He speaks to us through good men, through
good books, most loudly and explicitly through
our own experience.   To many their first clear
sense of God's presence has come through the
example or remonstrance of a friend or through
some awakening incident in life.   Far more

legibly and more convincingly than in Scripture do we read in our own experience some of
the profoundest and most salutary lessons God
has taught us.   Not *all* God's word is Scripture.   The spirit of God is not imprisoned in
the Bible nor limited by it.   As already noticed,
Romanists and the Friends are right in resolutely maintaining that the Spirit is ever alive
and active in the imparting of truth.

Yet among all words of God Scripture holds
a distinctive, an authoritative, a normative
position of its own.   What, then, is the difference ?   What is that which gives meaning to
our words when we call the Bible distinctively
the word of God?   While we acknowledge that
the same Spirit speaks to us through the words
and writings and lives of all good men, why do
we set Scripture apart from them all and assign
to it a place of supremacy ?   We do so *because
those books which form our Bible are all in direct
connection with God's historical revelation which
culminated in Christ.*   It is this alone which
gives to the Bible its normative character and
separates it from all other literature.   It is this
alone which forms the essential bond, the unifying element, in the books which form our
Canon.   In some of its parts, in the prophetic
books, in the recorded utterances of our Lord,

*But Scrip-
ture is the
word of
God.*

and so forth, the Bible is the very organ of God's revelation of Himself in that objective, historical line that was consummated in Christ; and in all its parts, if it is not the immediate organ of that revelation, then it is its record or its result and product. It is from Christ the central light that illuminating rays are shed through the whole of Scripture; He is the central sun who holds together all its various parts. It is in the Bible we find that word of God which it concerns all men to hear. It is in it that we listen to what God has to say to His children on earth as a society or Church. Here we have the public, common revelation, from which all Christian institutions and all Christian hopes spring and in which all Christians can meet.

Bible contains the consummate revelation of God.

This is a point which perhaps should be emphasized, as it seems to be so often missed by the great writers who influence our thoughts. Goethe, *e.g.*, in writing to Lavater says: " *You* find nothing more beautiful than the Gospel; I find a thousand pages written by both ancient and modern men, graciously endowed of God, as beautiful and useful and necessary to mankind." Mazzini, too, exclaims: "No! Eternal God! Thy word is not all fulfilled; Thy thought, the thought of the world, not all revealed. That thought creates still, and will continue to create for ages incalculable by man." And most impressive of all are Lowell's words : —

> " Slowly the Bible of the race is writ
> And not on paper leaves nor leaves of stone ;
> Each age, each kindred, adds to it,
> Texts of despair or hope, of joy or moan.
> While swings the sea, while mists the mountains shroud,
> While thunder's surges burst on cliffs of cloud,
> Still at the prophets' feet the nations sit."

The omitted idea in all these and a hundred similar utterances is that, though not closed, God's revelation is consummated in Christ; and that as all that went before prepared for that revelation, so all that follows illustrates, unfolds, and applies it, and must be judged by it. It is absurd to take the Bible piecemeal and declare that out of Shakespeare you can bring wisdom as profound and as helpful as anything in Proverbs, or that there are passages in Thomas à Kempis or Augustine or Bunyan which are as truly from God as anything in the Song of Songs. The value of the Bible results from its connection with Christ. He is the supreme, ultimate revelation of God, and the Bible, being the amber in which He is preserved for man, is as inviolable and unique

as He.   On all hands and in all ages there has
been knowledge of God.   He has never and nowhere left Himself without a witness: through
nature and through conscience and through the
experience of the misery that follows sin God
has spoken to men in general and to the individual in a language that many have been unable to misunderstand.   But all such revelation
is demonstrably incomplete without Christ.   It
is only in that crowning revelation that all becomes clear and that God is fully known.   It
cannot be too often repeated that the element
in the Bible which differentiates it is not the
supreme and unrivalled excellence of all its
constituent parts, nor that in it alone God
speaks to man, but that it is the record of His
supreme manifestation in Jesus Christ.

*This the
unifying
element.*

It is here, then, that we find the key to the
secret of the unifying element which has
brought these books together and which justi-
fies their elevation to the rank of a Canon of
Scripture.   And this key, as was to be expected, is not any accident of language, nor
any quality which these writings possess in
common with many others, but the essential
characteristic, the very meaning and substance
of the books.   Prior to Scripture, and underlying it, is God's revelation of Himself in and

to Israel. The Bible gives us an inspired utterance, record, and interpretation of this revelation. It is primarily the record of God's manifestation of Himself in history as winning and ruling men. Its unity is to be found in the unity of God's purpose. Or it may be said that its unity is to be found in its centre, Jesus Christ. In Him is the supreme manifestation of God; He is the culminating, unique revelation of God, and in Him the Bible finds its unity. It is either the record of His life, the transcript of His revelation and its interpretation, or it is the promise and preparation for His life, illustrating how greatly men needed this revelation, and tracing the steps by which at last the crowning manifestation became possible. Each part of Scripture receives its place and function by its relation to Jesus Christ.

II

THE CANON OF SCRIPTURE

II

THE CANON OF SCRIPTURE

THE readiest way to reach an intelligible and defensible position regarding the Canon is to trace the course of reasoning into which Luther was driven by his controversy with Rome.

If you ask a Romanist why he accepts certain books as canonical, he has a perfectly intelligible answer ready. He accepts these books because the Church bids him do so. The Church has determined what books are canonical, and he accepts the decision of the Church. If you ask a Protestant why he believes that just these books bound up together in his Bible are canonical, and neither more nor fewer, I fear that ninety-nine Protestants out of a hundred could give you no answer that would satisfy a reasonable man. The Protestant scorns the Romanist because he relies on the authority of the Church, but he cannot tell you on what authority he himself relies. The Protestant watchword is, "The Bible, the whole Bible,

Romanist and Protestant on Canon.

and nothing but the Bible," but how many
Protestants are there who could make it quite
clear that within the boards of their Bible they
have the whole Bible and nothing but the Bible?
If you asked them to show you that no canonical writing has been omitted, and that no un-
canonical writing has been received, how will
they proceed to do so? If you ask the average
Protestant to say why he receives the second
Epistle of Peter, which a large part of the
early Church declined to receive, or why he
accepts the Epistle of James, regarding which
Luther himself was more than doubtful, — what
can he say but that the Church to which he
belongs receives them? In other words, what
is the difference between the Protestant and
the Romanist on this cardinal point of canonicity? Do not Protestants and Romanists alike
accept their canonical books at the hands of
the Church?

*Council of
Trent's
decree.*

Let us see if any light can be shed on this
matter. And first of all, it may be well briefly
to indicate the position which the Church of
Rome assumed regarding the Canon at the
Reformation. Before the Council of Trent
there were laid four propositions which summed
up the heresy of Luther. Two of these concerned the Bible; the first being that Scripture

was the sole and complete source of doctrine;
the second, that the Hebrew Canon of the Old
Testament and the acknowledged books of the
New Testament should alone be admitted as
authoritative. In April, 1546, the Council,
after considerable debate, issued the following
decree: "The Holy, Œcumenical, and general
Synod of Trent legitimately convened in the
Holy Ghost . . . and having always as its
aim to remove errors and preserve the very
purity of the Gospel, which was promised before by the Prophets, and in the Holy Scripture, and which our Lord Jesus Christ, the
Son of God, first proclaimed with His own
lips, and then commanded to be preached by
His Apostles to every creature as the fountain
of all verity and saving truth, as well as of
instruction in conduct, and [this Council] perceiving that this truth and discipline are contained in written books, and in unwritten
traditions received by the Apostles from the
mouth of Christ Himself, or dictated to the
Apostles by the Holy Spirit, and handed down
as if from hand to hand even to us; following
the example of the Orthodox Fathers [this
Council] receives and venerates with an equal
piety and reverence all the books as well of
the Old as of the New Testament; one God

being the Author of both, together with the
Traditions pertaining both to faith and to
morals, as proceeding from the mouth of
Christ, or dictated by the Holy Spirit, and
preserved in the Church Catholic by continuous succession. And that no doubt may arise
as to what these books are which the Synod
thus receives, it has seemed good to append
to this decree a Catalogue of the Sacred
Books." Then follows a list which includes
the books of the Old Testament and the Apocrypha, and all the books now composing our
New Testament. And the Decree concludes
with an anathema on all who shall not receive
as sacred and canonical these books and all
their parts, "as they have been wont to be
read in the Church, and as they are contained
in the old vulgate Latin edition."

*This decree
a new de-
parture.*

Councils had previously taken the subject
of the Canon into consideration, and had pronounced upon it; but these councils were not
œcumenical and their decisions were not regarded. In fact, the very circumstance that
the Council of Trent found itself compelled to
give a definite decision on the subject suggests that there was no previous decree to which
they could appeal. Hitherto *usage* had determined the Canon. It was the universal use

of Jerome's Latin version, the Vulgate, which practically led the entire Western Church to adopt the same canon. But in the original admission of books into the Vulgate, Jerome did not carry through any scientific principle. He allowed himself to be guided by the generally received opinion, preferring the opinion of the primitive Church to that of a later date, and following the majority in preference to the minority.

Previous to the Reformation, then, the question of the Canon was in abeyance. The Church rested in the practical determination of the question by Jerome's issue of a Latin Bible which was everywhere received and used. And it was determined by Jerome with a regard to prevalent opinion in the Church, and not by the thorough application of a principle or test of canonicity, although no doubt underlying the procedure, both of the Church and of Jerome, there was the principle that those writings were canonical which proceeded from the Apostolic Circle. This principle had been explicitly enounced by Tertullian, and it was only the difficulty of making good the claims of certain writings to be of Apostolic origin that prevented them from being universally accepted as canonical.

Canon hitherto determined by the Vulgate.

This had hitherto sufficed.

This practical solution of the difficulty worked very well as long as the Bible was merely used as a book of edification, or to eke out a Church service.   But when Luther and his followers proposed to make it the one law of everything religious and ecclesiastical; when they proposed on its authority to repudiate and condemn what was imposed upon them by the authority of the Church; when they proposed to listen to it, not as a law which must be interpreted and modified by other laws, but as the one only rule of faith and life, — then it became necessary to define with precision what writings contained this law and whence they derived their authority.   In answering these questions the Church of Rome found no difficulty.   Even before the Council of Trent was convened, one of her theologians had asked, "How can you know that the Scriptures are canonical except by the Church?"   Another had said, "The whole authority which the Scripture has among us necessarily depends upon the authority of the Church."   "It is the Church which has invested with authority certain books . . . which did not derive this authority either from themselves or from their authors."   When Luther objected to Eck's citing a passage from Second Maccabees to prove the doctrine of Purgatory,

Eck replied, "But the Church has received these books into the Canon." To which Luther answered : "The Church cannot give more authority or force to a book than it has in itself. A Council cannot make that be Scripture which in its own nature is not Scripture."[1]

These quotations sufficiently show the dia- *Luther was* metrical contradiction between the position of *compelled to* Luther and that of the Romanists. The Church *exact.* of Rome decreed that the Old Testament books (both those we receive and those called Apocryphal), and the books of the New Testament as we now have them, be received as Scripture. They instituted no further inquiries into their authenticity ; they simply closed all debate regarding this matter by accepting Jerome's Vulgate. With Luther such an easy course was impossible. Denying the authority of the Church, he was compelled to define clearly the authority on which he rested. Claiming the words of God as his sole authority, he must set forth with distinctness where the Word of God is to be found and how he can recognize it to be the Word of God. There were two ques- *and asks* tions which Luther found himself driven to *two questions.* answer : What assures me that Scripture is the Word of God, and therefore authoritative? and,

[1] C. Berger, "Histoire de la Vulgate," p. 86.

What books are Scripture?   Prior to the question, What is the Canon of inspired Scripture? comes the question, Is there an inspired Scripture?   Prior to the question, What writings contain the Word of God? comes the question, Is there a Word of God?   We cannot understand Luther's answer to the one question unless we recognize his attitude toward the other.

Is there a Word of God?

Now, according to Luther, the prior question, Is there a Word of God? or, Has God spoken? is answered in the affirmative, and with certainty, by every man in whom the Word of God attests its own Divine origin and authority, and it can be answered with an assured affirmative by none beside.   Luther's explicit and constant teaching is that this word is self-evidencing and needs no authority at its back, but carries in it its own authentication.   Let us hear some of his own strong statements to this effect.   Showing that the question between himself and Rome was not whether God was to be obeyed when He spoke, — for they were agreed as to that, — he goes on: " The Romanists say, Yes, but how can we know what is God's Word, and what is true or false?   We must learn it from the Pope and the Councils.   Very well, let them decree and say what they will, still say I, Thou can'st not rest thy confidence thereon, nor satisfy thy conscience : thou must thyself decide, thy neck is at stake, thy life is at stake. Therefore must GOD say to thee in thine heart, This is God's Word, else it is still undecided." Again : " Thou must be as certain that it is the Word of God as thou art certain that thou livest, and even more certain, for on this alone must thy conscience rest. And even if all men came, aye, even the angels and all the world, and determined something, if THOU can'st not form nor conclude the decision, thou art lost. For thou must not place thy decision on the Pope or any other, thou must thyself be so skilful that thou can'st say, God says this, not that; this is right, that is wrong; else it is not possible to endure. Dost thou stand upon Pope or Concilia? Then the Devil may at once knock a hole in thee and insinuate, ' How if it were false, how if they have erred ? ' Then thou art laid low at once. Therefore thou must bring *conscience* into play, that thou may'st boldly and defiantly say, That is God's Word, on that will I risk body and life, and a hundred thousand necks if I had them. Therefore no one shall turn me from the Word which GOD teaches me, and that must I know as certainly as that two and three make five, that an ell is longer than a

half. That is certain, and though all the world
speak to the contrary, still I know that it is
not otherwise. Who decides me there? No
man, but only THE TRUTH which is so perfectly
certain that nobody can deny it."

Self-evidenc-
ing Word of
God the
basis of
Protestant-
ism.

Why is Luther so urgent on this point?
He is urgent because he sees that the whole
difference between himself and Rome hinges
here. If he cannot make good this position,
that the truth or the Word of God has power
to verify itself as such to the conscience it
awakens, he has no standing at all. The principle which made him a Protestant, and which
constitutes men Protestants always, is simply
this, that the soul needs not the intervention
of any authority to bring it into contact with
God and the truth, but that God and His truth
have power to verify themselves to the individual. Luther did not accept the Gospel
because it was written in a book he believed
to be inspired, or canonical, or the Word of
God; but he accepted it because it brought
new life to his spirit and proved itself to be
from God. He did not accept Christ because
he had first of all accepted the Scriptures, but
he accepted the Scriptures because they testi-
fied of a Christ he felt constrained to accept.
In short, it is the truth which the Scriptures

contain which certify him that they are the
Word of God; it is not his belief that they
are the Word of God which certifies him of
the truth they contain. The proclamation of
God's grace quickening a new life within him
convinced him this proclamation was from
God.

The difference between the Romanist and *Differentia*
the Protestant is not what it is so often said *of Protes-*
to be, that the Romanist accepts the Church *tantism.*
as his infallible authority, while the Protestant
accepts the Scriptures as his infallible authority. The Romanist equally with the Protestant
accepts the authority of Scripture. The difference lies deeper. The difference lies here:
that the Romanist accepts Scripture as the
Word of God because the Church tells him
so, the Protestant accepts it as the Word of
God because God tells him so. The Protestant
believes it to be God's Word because through
it God has spoken to him in such sort as to
convince him that it is God who here speaks.
This is the one sure foundation-stone of Protestantism, — the response of the individual conscience to the self-evidencing voice of God in
Scripture. He does not need to go to the
Church to ask if this be God's Word; his conscience tells him it is. Deeper than that for a

foundation of faith you cannot get, and any faith that is not so deeply founded is insecure — it may last, and it may bring a man to all needed benefit, but it is not reasonably defensible, and therefore it is liable to be upset.

This, then, was Luther's first position regarding Scripture ; this was the fundamental position on which Protestantism is reared ; viz. that through Scripture God Himself so speaks to the soul that the man is convinced without the intervention of any other proof or authority that this is the Word of God. The individual does not need the Church to tell him that this is the Word of God. God tells him so, and makes all other authority superfluous.

What writings contain God's Word?

But next comes the question, What writings contain this word? Are we to carry through this fundamental principle, and maintain that only such writings can be accounted Scripture as approve themselves to be God's Word by renewing or building up the fundamental faith in God which has already been quickened within us? This fundamental principle of Protestantism — that God's Word is self-evidencing — can we carry it over to the subject of canonicity and make it the sole, absolute test of canonicity? Or can we at any rate say that whatever agrees with the Word of God which

at first begot faith in us and presents to us the
same Gospel and the same Christ is canonical?
This Luther does, subject to the limitation that
it springs from the Apostolic Circle. Or can
we only use this fundamental faith of our own
as a negative test, rejecting whatever does *not
harmonize* with that faith in Christ which has
given us spiritual life, or at any rate whatever
contradicts it? In other words, can I say that
all those writings are canonical which awaken
faith in me, or can I say that all those writings are canonical which present that same
Christ whose presentation at first awakened
faith in me; or can I only say that those are
certainly not canonical which do not harmonize
with faith in Christ?

Now we shall find Luther's answer to these
questions in the judgments he pronounced on
the books actually forming our Canon. Taking up his translation of the New Testament,
we find that the four writings — Hebrews,
James, Jude, and Revelation — which he considered to be non-apostolic, are relegated to
the end by themselves, and introduced with
these significant words: " Up to this point we
have been dealing with the quite certain (*rech-
ten gewissen*) chief books (*Hauptbücher*) of the
New Testament. But these four following

Luther's answer.

have in times past had a different position."
He then goes on to prove briefly but convincingly that Hebrews is not by Paul nor by any
Apostle, and after extolling its ability and
pointing out what he considered faulty, he
remarks that "although the writer does not
lay the *foundation* of faith, which is the Apostolic function, he yet builds upon it gold,
silver, precious stones, and if, in accordance
with Paul's words, he mingles some wood, hay,
stubble, this is not to hinder us from accepting
with all reverence his teaching — although it
cannot in all respects be compared to the Apostolic Epistles." His criticisms on the Apocalypse are also very outspoken: "My spirit,"
he says, "can't accommodate itself to this
book : *the reason being that I do not think Christ
is taught therein.*" [1] His judgment of this
book, however, underwent considerable modification; and although, in contradistinction to
the body of modern critics, he seems never to
have been convinced that it was written by the
Apostle John, it is not probable that in his
later years he would have spoken of it so slight-
ingly. But in his introductory remarks to the

[1] Luther's " Prefaces " are to be found in old editions of
his translation of the Bible. See also Reuss's " Histoire du
Canon," p. 347.

Epistle of James he shows more explicitly his criterion or test of canonicity. He refuses to admit this Epistle among the *Hauptbücher* of the New Testament, or to allow its Apostolic authorship, and he defends his judgment in these words: " Herein agree all the genuine (*rechtschaffene*) holy books, that they all preach and exhibit Christ. This, indeed, is the right touchstone (*der rechte Prüfestein*) to test all the books, — if one sees whether or not they present Christ, for all Scripture witnesses to Christ (Rom. iii. 21); and St. Paul will know nothing but Christ. That which does not teach Christ is not Apostolic, though St. Peter or St. Paul teaches it. That which preaches Christ is Apostolic, though Judas, Annas, Pilate, or Herod teaches it."

Luther's test of canonicity.

Luther's direct test of canonicity, then, is, Does the book in question occupy itself with Christ or does it not? So says Dorner:[1] " The deciding principle as to whether a writing is to pass for canonical, lies, in a dogmatic aspect, according to Luther, as is well known, in this, whether it is occupied with Christ." Luther, in short, recognizes that God has an end to secure in making a revelation, and this end is to bring clear before men His will for

[1] " History of Protestant Theology," E. Tr., I., p. 252.

our salvation; or, in one word, Christ. The
books that promote this end he accepts as
canonical.

Its inade-
quacy.
But while this was Luther's final and determining test of canonicity, it is obvious that he
at the same time employed some preliminary
test.   He applied his final test, not to all books
he knew, but only to a number already selected
and already passing for canonical.   He never
thought of carrying his principle through all
literature and accepting as canonical every
book that was occupied with Christ.   He did
not accept Augustine and Tauler as canonical,
though to them he in great part owed his
salvation, his peace, his light, his strength.
And it may, on the other hand, be questioned
whether, with all his boldness, he would have
dared to reject any writing which was proved
to be of Apostolic authorship.   In point of fact
he does *not* reject any such writing.   His test
of canonicity is, in short, only a supplemental
principle; it is a principle which can be applied
only in a field already defined by the application of some other principle, or by some universal usage such as the Church-collection of
Scriptures had sprung from.   Luther's method
is really this : he first accepts at the hand of
Jerome certain candidates for admission into

the Canon, and to these selected candidates he applies his test. He was aware that up to Jerome's time the Church had always been in doubt regarding certain of these writings, and to these he freely applies the testing question, Are they occupied with Christ?

Theoretically, therefore, Reuss is right in say- *Reuss on* ing that Luther did not look upon the Canon *Luther.* as a collection, more or less complete, of all the writings of a certain period or of a certain class of men, but as a body of writings destined by God *to teach a certain truth;* and accordingly the test of the individual writings must at bottom lie in the teaching itself.[1] But *practically* what Luther did was to apply this test only to writings which already had some claim to be considered Apostolical. The course of his thought was briefly this : he arrived at faith in Christ before he reached any clear view of the inspiration or canonicity of certain writers ; he reached faith in Christ apart from any doctrine regarding Scripture. But having believed in Christ, he found that certain men had been appointed by Christ to witness to the great facts of His life, death, resurrection, and gift of the Spirit. The same faith which accepts Christ as supreme, the same faith which

[1] " History of Protestant Theology," E. Tr., I., p. 344.

produces self-verifying results in his soul, compels him also to believe that the commission of Christ to His Apostles was actually effectual and that they are the appointed, normative witnesses to Him and His salvation. The writings of these Apostles he accepts, though holding himself free to reject them if they contradict the fundamental faith in Christ which gave him his new life. The other books, whose authorship is doubtful, but which from the first have claimed admittance to the New Testament Canon, he judges purely on their merits, rejecting or admitting as he finds they do not or do fit into the Apostolic teaching.

Liberty allowed by Luther.

This, it will be said, leaves a ragged edge on the Canon. It leaves much to be decided by the individual. A man may say to Luther, "I do not find in the gospel of John agreement with the three synoptic gospels, and as you throw over James because he does not agree with Paul, so I throw over John because he does not agree with the synoptists." And Luther could have made no satisfactory reply. Better, he would think, let a man accept Scripture from his own feeling of its truth than compel him to do so by some external compulsion. Indeed, his boldness in pronouncing his own opinion is quite equalled by his explicit and repeated allowance of liberty to every other man. Thus, though he himself did not accept the Apocalypse as the work of John, he hastens to add, "No man ought to be hindered from holding it to be a work of St. John or otherwise as he will." Similarly, after giving his opinion of the Epistle of James, he concludes, "I cannot then place it among the chief books, but I will forbid no one to place and elevate it as he pleases." So that if we find ourselves in disagreement with Luther regarding the judgments he pronounces on some of the books of Scripture, this is only what he himself anticipated. Neither does the fact that his principle can never be applied without such discordant results emerging, reflect any discredit on the principle itself. As Reuss says, "To begin to speak to-day of the infatuation of Luther's method of procedure, because in the details of its application one cannot always share in his opinion, this only proves that with the modern champions of a pretended, privileged orthodoxy, ignorance and fatuity go hand and hand in the van."

The same vagueness which marred the Lutheran doctrine of canonicity affected the Calvinistic position. The inward witness cannot reasonably be expected to be sufficient for the

Calvinistic position.

task of certifying every word that God has uttered to man. It cannot, in other words, be expected to form of itself a sufficient test of canonicity.

Confusion of thought regarding Canon.

The truth is there seems to have been some confusion of thought in Calvinistic writers, arising from the fact that in speaking of the *authority* of Scripture they viewed Scripture *as a whole*. Challenged by the Romanists to say how they knew the Bible to be from God, they said, We know it to be from God because God's Spirit within us recognizes it as His. But this inward witness could only become a test of canonicity if the Bible were an indissoluble whole, part hanging with part, so that each part stands or falls with every other part.

Inadequacy of inward witness.

If, in order to prove the canonicity of *all* the writings in the Bible, it were enough to say, the Spirit within me recognizes God's voice in the Bible as a whole, then this were a sufficient test. If, in order to prove the canonicity of the Epistle of James, it were enough to say, I recognize the voice of God in the Epistle of John, then the " inward witness of the Spirit " would be a sufficient test. But the very thing we are seeking for is *that which brought the parts together*, the principle on which the Church proceeded when it took one writing here and

another there and brought them into one whole.
What is it which is characteristic of each part,
so that even when the parts were lying separate, they could be and were recognized as
properly belonging to the Canonical Scriptures?
The question seeking solution is, why do we receive this or that book into the Canon? There
is no question here as to whether we have a
word of God, nor as to the *general* collection of
writings in which we find that word; the question is, how do we know that the Epistle to the
Hebrews or the Epistle of Jude, or any other
individual writing, is the Word of God?

The Westminster Confession makes "inspiration" the test of canonicity, although it does
not in express terms say so. After naming the
books of the Old and New Testament, it proceeds, "all which are given by inspiration of
God;" and then in section 3 it goes on, "The
books commonly called Apocrypha, *not being of
Divine inspiration*, are no part of the Canon of
Scripture." That is to say, writings which are
inspired are canonical, writings not inspired are
not canonical. But how are we to discover
what writings are inspired? The Confession,
singularly enough, says nothing of Prophetic
and Apostolic authorship, but refers us to the
various marks of divinity in the writings them-

*Can inspira-
tion be the
test of can-
onicity?*

selves, and concludes in the well-known words, "Our full persuasion and assurance of the infallible truth and Divine authority thereof, is from the inward work of the Holy Spirit, bearing witness by and with the word in our hearts."

How can inspiration be recognized?

There are two processes by which we can arrive at the conclusion that a writing is inspired. First, as in reading any book we form an opinion of it and either pronounce it stupid or feel in it the touch of genius, so in reading the work of an inspired man we may arrive at the conclusion that it has been written with Divine aid. There may be that in it which makes us feel that we have to do with a Divine as well as a human author. Second, we may believe in the inspiration of a book, because we first of all believe in Christ and find that He authorized certain persons to speak in His name and with His authority and spirit. When the well-authenticated writings of such persons come into our hands, we accept them, if we are already Christian.

Inspiration not always recognizable.

But there are books in the Bible whose inspiration cannot be ascertained by either of these methods. There are books of which we cannot say that they are written by prophet or apostle or otherwise commissioned person; Chronicles, Esther, Job, Ecclesiastes, — no one knows who wrote these books. One of the methods of ascertaining inspiration is therefore closed to us. And as to the other method, the inward witness, I am not persuaded that John Owen himself could have detected the book of Esther as an inspired book, had it been found lying outside the Canon. How, then, can we justify the admission of such a book as Esther — a book of which the authorship is unknown, and to which the inward witness bears at the best a somewhat doubtful testimony so far as regards its inspiration?

To say that we accept it because the Jews accepted it, is simply to fall back to the Romanist position and take our Canon at the hands and by the authority of the Church. To affirm that the men who settled the Canon were inspired, is to assume what cannot be proved, and even to affirm what we know to be false, because discussion was still going on among the Jews regarding their Canon as late as the year 96 A.D. We can only justify the admission of these books on some such general ground as that of Luther — their congruity to the main end of revelation. If by "canonical writings" we mean the writings through which God conveys to us the knowledge of the revelation He has made, if this be the prominent

True test of canonicity.

idea, and if their being the rule of faith and life be an inference from this, then we get a broader basis for the Canon and can admit into it all writings which have a direct connection with God's revelation of Himself in Christ. If the book in question gives us a link in the history of that revelation, or if it represents a stage of God's dealings and of the growth His people had made under these dealings, and if it contains nothing which is quite inconsistent with the idea of its being inspired, then its claim to be admitted seems valid. Therefore I would be disposed to say that the two attributes which give canonicity are congruity with the main end of revelation and direct historical connection with the revelation of God in history.[1]

All canonical Scriptures not equally important.

It may indeed be said that if such a book as Esther were lost, nothing that is *essential* to the history would be lost, or that if several of the Psalms were lost nothing essential would be lost. But this is really to say no more than that a man who has lost a joint of a finger or a toe has lost nothing *essential*. No doubt he can live on and do his work, but he is not a complete man. And there are parts of the body of

[1] A similar, if not identical, conclusion was reached by the late A. B. Bruce, but I have lost the reference.

which it is very difficult to say why they are there, or why they are of the particular form they are; but there they are, and the want of them would seem a deformity. So of the Bible, we may not be able to say of every part what is its exact relation to the whole; nor yet may we be able in honesty to say that we think anything essential would be lost were certain portions of Scripture to be removed; and yet he would be a rash man who would dare to aver that he could improve upon the Canon, or who should think it needful to excise from it such parts as to himself may seem unimportant.

From all this, then, we must gather (1) that churches should be cautious in speaking of the Canon as an absolutely defined collection of writings, thoroughly and to a nicety ascertained, based on distinct principles and precisely separated at every point from all extracanonical literature. There is no reasonable doubt that the bulk of the books of the New Testament come to us so accredited that to reject them is equivalent to rejecting the authority of Christ; but a few are not so accredited, and it is a question whether our creeds ought not to reflect the fact that in the early Church some books were universally admitted into the Canon, while regarding seven of the books of our New

Canon not absolutely definite.

Testament grave doubts were entertained. The position taken by one of the greatest champions of Protestantism, Chillingworth, is one that commends itself: " I *may* believe even those questioned books to have been written by the Apostles and to be canonical; but I cannot in reason believe this of them so undoubtedly as of those books which were never questioned: at least I have no warrant to damn any man that shall doubt of them or deny them now, having the example of saints in heaven, either to justify or excuse such their doubting or denial." This was the position of Luther and of the Reformers generally, and for my part I think it a pity it was ever abandoned. It is not a calamity over which one need make great moan, but unquestionably the combining of less authenticated books with those that are thoroughly authenticated has rather tended to bring the latter class under suspicion with persons ignorant of their history.

Proper attitude of lay Protestant. We also gather (2) what ought to be the attitude of the ordinary, lay Protestant toward this subject of the Canon. Sometimes Romanists have taunted us with the absurdity of inviting each Protestant, educated or uneducated, to settle the Canon for himself. The taunt is based on a misconception. It is the

right of every Protestant to inquire into the
evidence on which certain books are received as
canonical, and the more that right is exercised,
the better. But even when the right is not used,
it is not thereby resigned. Protestants receive
the Canon as they receive historical facts, on
the testimony of those who have pursued this
line of inquiry. We may never have individually looked into the evidence for Alexander's
invasion of India, but we take it on the word
of those best informed regarding historical matters, reserving of course the right to examine
it ourselves if need arises. So on this subject
of the Canon, the lay Protestant accepts the
judgment of the Reformed Churches, feeling
tolerably confident that after all the research
and discussion which learned men have spent
upon this subject, the results cannot be seriously misleading. But he of course reserves
the right to inquire for himself if opportunity
should arise, and does not dream that the decision of the Church binds him to accept certain
books as Divine. The Protestant accepts the
decision of the Church precisely as he accepts
the decision of engineers or medical men or
experts of any kind in their respective departments — he accepts it as the result arrived at
after deliberation by competent men. The

Romanist accepts the decision of the Church
as a decree or law issued because the Church
wills it so, and not as the mere finding of learned
men ; and the Romanist has no right to revise
the Church's decision. The Romanist holds
that the Church has power to make books
canonical ; the Protestant holds that irrespective of any ecclesiastical decision there is that
in the books themselves which makes them
canonical. To confound the two positions is
ignorant or malicious.

*Investiga-
tion invited.*
(3) Again, Protestants are taunted with the
diversity of opinion consequent on leaving such
questions to individual research and private
judgment. I reply that it is a vast advantage
so to leave such questions, for it is to invite
investigation, and to invite investigation is to
secure that one day the truth will shine in the
eye of the world. What value attaches to the
unanimity that is secured by closing every one's
eyes, and shutting every one's mouth? That
unanimity alone is valuable which the truth
itself commands. And this unanimity can only
be attained by diligent, reverent, truth-seeking
investigation. For my part, I think Luther
was right in holding that regarding some of
the books there must be difference of opinion
always ; but of the great bulk of the New Testa-

ment, — the four Gospels, the Acts, the Epistles of Paul, the First of Peter, and the First of John, — as there was no difference of opinion in the early Church, so eventually there will be entire agreement. Men do not differ regarding the authorship of " Hamlet," nor the esteem in which that writing should be held, neither will private judgment and liberty of criticism cause men to differ regarding the canonical books, but will rather bring them to the only agreement that is worth having.

Lastly, let us remember that the true Protestant order is, first, faith in Christ; second, faith in Scripture. Our faith in Christ does not hang upon our faith in Scripture, but our faith in Scripture hangs upon our faith in Christ. Our faith in Christ may depend on Scripture as a true history; but not as an inspired canonical book. It is Christ as presented in Scripture or by other means, by preaching as in the first age, and often now, that evokes faith. He and he only is the true Protestant who knows that God has spoken to him in Christ, and who knows this irrespective of any infallible authority separable from Christ himself, whether that authority be the authority of the Church or the authority of Scripture. We must not shift the ultimate authority from Christ to Scripture.

Christ the ultimate authority.

III

REVELATION

III

REVELATION

IF the Bible is *the* word of God *par excellence*, because it is the organ and record of the revelation of Himself which God has given in history, we shall understand the Bible better if we endeavor to ascertain what we can regarding revelation. It is a subject full of difficulty, obscured and perplexed by many controversies, and on which light is only slowly rising. Avoiding as far as possible the entanglement of needless discussions, we may consider (1) What is meant by revelation ; (2) Whether it is possible; (3) Whether any revelation has actually been made, and where ; (4) The method that has been pursued ; and (5) The purpose in view.

The Bible record a revelation.

1. First, we must understand what we mean when we use the word " revelation," for it has been and is used in different senses. Sometimes it is used to denote the immediate communication of truth to the mind, as when Paul affirms that it was by revelation of Jesus Christ he had received his gospel. Sometimes it is

Meaning of the word " revelation."

used of the external manifestation or event
through which truth reaches the mind, as the
Flood is spoken of as a revelation of the righteousness of God.   Sometimes it is used of the
truth revealed.   The distinction which pre-
vailed during the eighteenth century between
natural and revealed religion imposed a special
meaning upon the word "revelation," and it
was used to denote the knowledge of God which
comes to us not through nature, but through
some special and supernatural action of God.
Thus Butler says : "Some persons upon pretence of the sufficiency of the light of nature
avowedly reject all revelation, as, in its very
nature, incredible, and what must be fictitious.
And indeed it is certain no revelation would
have been given, had the light of nature been
sufficient in such a sense as to render one not
wanting and useless."   The term "revelation"
is thus exclusively applied to Christianity, and
Judaism as preliminary to it ; and is therefore
and with some confusion of thought applied to
the Bible itself as containing the substance and
history of this revelation.

*Its proper
use.*

But this use of the word is unfortunate.
For it assumes that God has not revealed Himself to any who are beyond the pale of Christianity, that He has not revealed Himself in

creation, and has actually left Himself without a witness save in Jewish and Christian circles. The distinction between Christianity and other religions would be better expressed by the terms "perfect" and "imperfect" or "final" and "preparatory" than by "revealed" and "natural." For at the basis of every religion there is necessarily some knowledge of God, however slender; and this knowledge of God can only be of a God who has somehow revealed Himself. There is a great and profound truth in Pascal's words put into God's mouth : "Thou wouldest not seek Me, hadst thou not already found Me." All the feelings after God which are seen in the various races of mankind are evidence that God has been revealing Himself to them. Revelation, then, should be kept in its full and proper sense and be used to denote God's making Himself known to man, whether in the natural order or through what is supernatural, whether with greater and more convincing clearness or with dim intimations of His presence.

Another erroneous view of revelation, also current during the eighteenth century, was that it meant the communication of certain truths to the human mind — truths which the human mind of itself could not reach, or could not so

Not the communication of certain truths.

quickly reach. This was due to the pedantic and
elaborate dogmatism of the seventeenth century.
The Bible had so persistently been used as a
text-book to prove dogma that this came to be
considered its main use, and it was never questioned whether some higher purpose was not
meant to be served by it. Revelation was
identified with the Bible, and it was taken for
granted that the purpose of revelation was to
impart truth. There was great difference of
opinion as to the need of this Divine instruction
and as to its contents. Some supposed that in
the Bible all knowledge was to be found ; that
scientific and metaphysical mysteries were hidden in its pages. Each of its utterances, no
matter in what department of truth, was supposed to be final and authoritative. " Who,"
said Calovius, " would dare to set the authority
of Copernicus above the authority of God ? "
Others limited the pædagogic function of Scriptures to the communication of truths regarding
God, immortality, and duty. The Westminster Shorter Catechism, to the question, What
do the Scriptures principally teach ? replies
very wisely, " The Scriptures principally teach
what man is to believe concerning God and
what duty God requires of man." Nothing
could be better as an answer to the question,

but nowadays such a question would not be the first or only one about Scripture. Scripture is no longer looked upon as a lesson-book.

One has only to look at the Bible to see how singularly ill adapted it is to be a theological text-book. God's object throughout human history has evidently been not to make men theological experts, but to make Himself known. His purpose has not been to inform men regarding abstruse mysteries, free will, predestination, the future state, but to give them assurance of His own presence, and of His holiness and love. And what we have in the Bible, therefore, is not an inspired catechism nor a revealed creed, but a record of the great momenta of God's revelation of Himself. And Jesus Christ being that consummate revelation of God which absorbs and eclipses all others, the Bible may best be considered as either a preparation for or an exhibition and explanation of Jesus Christ.

The Bible not a theological text-book.

Revelation, then, is not exactly equivalent to the Bible; and although it might mean the communication of truth, and does involve the communication of truth, yet primarily, and properly, it means God's making Himself known to man.

2. *Possibility of Revelation.*—To discuss the possibility of revelation is needless. Theists of all schools, by the fact of their theism, admit

Revelation possible.

the possibility of revelation. They are theists because behind and beneath the world they discern a spirit in whom is life and purpose. Their fundamental belief is that through all with which we are in sensible contact in this life God makes Himself known. Paul indeed says that the world by wisdom knew not God. But by this he did not mean that it attained to no knowledge of God, but only that it did not reach a perfect knowledge such as we have in Christ. Max Müller, on the other hand, affirms that apart from Judaism and Christianity men have formed the highest conception of God. But this is the exaggeration of a man biassed by his favorite study. The world apart from Christ has not reached the highest conception of God, but it has recognized His existence and His presence. Theism is simply the declaration that this world cannot be rationally construed without the hypothesis of purpose and of a mind in which this purpose is formed and by which it is guided; that is to say, that God has revealed Himself in the constitution of the world and of man. The harmony of all nature and the tendency of its most various constituents toward one end are becoming daily more obvious, and theists maintain that this consistency of nature can be accounted for only on the supposition that it is governed by purpose. The instinctive persistency with which through all interruptions man cleaves to a moral ideal, never ceasing to have it in view and to work toward it, implies an existence superior to his own in which that ideal is actualized and which is the guarantee of his attainment. Chiefly in these two directions, in the harmony and progress of nature and also in man's moral ideal, theists maintain that God has revealed Himself.

On the other hand, to deny the possibility of revelation is to deny the possibility of religion or to declare it a delusion. "Of every religion," says Principal Fairbairn,[1] "the idea of revelation is an integral part ; the man who does not believe that God can speak to him will not speak to God." However hidden and incomprehensible the Divine Being is, there can be no religion, unless it is believed that there is a God, and consequently that somehow that God has made Himself known. And, moreover, to an absolutely silent God who in no way responds to man's yearning for fellowship with the Divine, and who gives no intimation of His presence by word or deed in the life or heart of His worshipper, homage must soon cease to be

No religion without revelation.

[1] "Christ in Modern Theology," p. 494.

paid.   As Professor Tiele [1] says, "It is certain that no communion of man with his God is possible or conceivable if all the aspirations of the pious soul, all its longings and entreaties for help, light, and support, are to end in the despairing cynicism of Heinrich Heine, 'No one but a fool expects an answer.'"   A religion that is entirely one-sided as surely falls to the ground as a one-sided bridge, or a bird that beats its wings in a vacuum.   The rudest fetich worship proceeds upon the assumption that the unseen has a will and can somehow express it.   The Greek who consulted the oracle, the Roman who waited for the augur's decisions, recognized that religion could not be one-sided, but that there must be Divine response to human inquiry.   And although often rudely enough conceived, the belief in God's power and desire to make Himself and His will known to men is sound and true.

Pfleiderer's argument.   *A priori*, it might justly be argued that spirits living in one another's presence and related to one another as are God and man, should be able to communicate with one another.   Pfleiderer in his "Philosophy of Religion" [2] argues thus: "Why should it be less possible for God to enter

[1] "Gifford Lectures," II., p. 157.
[2] III., p. 305, E. Tr.

into a loving fellowship with us than for men to do so with each other? I should be inclined to think that He is even more capable of doing so. For as no man can altogether read the soul of another, so no man can altogether live in the soul of another; hence all our human love is and remains imperfect. But if we are shut off from one another by the limits of individuality, in relation to God it is not so; to Him our hearts are as open as each man's heart is to himself; He sees through and through them, and desires to live in them, and to fill them with His own sacred energy and blessedness."

Others, again, have argued from the nature of personality that a Personal God must necessarily reveal Himself. Thus Mr. Illingworth has shown that love, desire for free intercourse with other persons, is an essential of personality. According to Mr. Illingworth's searching exposition there are three constituent elements of personality, — self-consciousness, the power of self-determination, and desires which irresistibly impel us into communion with other persons; or, in other words, reason, will, and love. "We are so constituted that we cannot regard inanimate property, uncommunicated knowledge, unreciprocated emotion, solitary action, otherwise than as

Illing-worth's argument.

means to an end. We press on through it
all till we have found persons like ourselves
with whom to share it, and then we are at
rest." "We require to find in other persons
an end in which our entire personality may
rest. And this is the relationship of love."
If God, then, is Personal, this essential element
of personality must appear in Him. He must
desire the existence of persons in whom His
nature can find satisfaction. And all who follow Mr. Illingworth's argument will agree with
his conclusion that "we cannot conceive a Person freely creating persons except with a view
to hold intercourse with them when created."

*Is direct
intercourse
with God
possible?*

Both Pfleiderer and Illingworth seem to
believe it possible for the Divine Spirit to
hold *direct* intercourse with the human spirit;
that is to say, that the Divine Spirit apart from
any means or media can come into contact with
the spirit of man and communicate of His fulness to him. And certainly there is much in
Scripture, if not in common experience, which
seems to justify this idea; although from the
nature of the case it is difficult to verify. It
is indeed at this point, the intercourse or con-
currence of the human and the Divine, that
the human mind so often finds itself baffled in
various directions of theological inquiry.

3. Has God revealed Himself, and where? *God re-vealed in creation.* Necessarily God has revealed Himself in His works. What He has created and what He has done manifest His character. There may or may not have been minds capable of apprehending this revelation, but none the less has the revelation been made. As you ascertain a man's existence and come to understand his character from his actions, so God, being ever present and ever operative in the world, necessarily manifests His existence and His nature. If all this vast universe, with its upholding laws and forces, and its endless variety of living forms, has sprung from the design and creative will of God, then what we see in the world around us cannot fail to show us something of the nature of God. The heavens declare the glory of God. There is much indeed that is difficult to interpret, — the cruelty, the pain that appear in all creation, — but at any rate we learn the magnitude of existence, the regularity and resistless power of its forces, and so come to some apprehension of the resource and unthinkable power of God. Slowly the idea of God has grown and expanded in the human mind as men have pondered this revelation of Himself in the world : many grotesque and dishonoring thoughts of Him have had their

day and been at last eliminated ; much has yet
to be learned from this manifestation of the
unseen Spirit in material works, but doubtless
the revelation is there for those who can understand it.

> " Of this fair volume which we world do name,
> If we the sheets and leaves could turn with care,
>   Of him who it corrects and did it frame,
>   We clear might read the art and wisdom rare :
> Find out his power which wildest powers doth tame,
>   His providence extending everywhere,
>   His justice which proud rebels doth not spare,
>   In every page, no period of the same,
> But silly we, like foolish children, rest
>   Well pleased with colored vellum, leaves of gold,
>   Fair dangling ribbons, leaving what is best,
>   On the great writer's sense ne'er taking hold ;
> Or if by chance we stay our minds on aught,
>   It is some picture on the margin wrought."
>   *—William Drummond (Hawthornden),*
>   *translated from Sonnet by Marino.*

*God re-
vealed in
man.*

But as the writer to the Hebrews reminds us,
God has "spoken," or revealed Himself "in
many ways." And the character of God is
more distinctly exhibited in the nature of man,
and in God's government of him in providence.
From man's recognition of his own moral
nature, his instinct to approve the good, his
admiration for what is heroic in self-sacrifice,
his homage to what is loving, he concludes the

nature of God, the source of all this, his Crea-
tor. As man grows in good, so grows his idea
of God. It is largely through his own efforts
after goodness and unaccomplishing instincts
for goodness that he perceives what God must
be. The best that is in him is surpassed, infinitely surpassed, by God; and as he himself,
under God's educating hand, grows to perceive
moral beauties and ideals that previously were
hidden from him, so he grows in wider and
truer thoughts of God. For it is still through
his own nature he conceives of God. As
Whittier puts it : —

> " By all that He requires of me
> I know what God Himself must be."

But the revelation of Himself, which prepared *In history.*
for God's manifestation in Christ, was especially
historical. It was through His dealings with
men in providence that His people learned to
know Him. The readiness of certain races to
perceive God may be gathered from the quick-
ness with which they deduced from the Flood
that God was a holy God. The instinct of
conscience was seen in their referring to their
own sins this devastating visitation. In that
event God conveyed to men the impression that
His holiness was genuine and essential. One

of the fundamental lessons which men could receive was then given, and it was given in a language suited to the times and intelligible to the dullest mind.   And all through the history of Israel, in the calamities that followed wrong-doing, in the disgrace and weakness that followed unfaithfulness to God, the people with always increasing clearness recognized that it was a righteous and gracious God who was governing them.   They got nearer and nearer to a true insight into His character, and this they did by means of the revelation He made of Himself in ordering the events which formed their history.

God revealed as Redeemer.

It is especially to be noticed that throughout the history of Israel God revealed Himself as a Redeemer, as a God who befriends His people on earth; thinking tenderest thoughts, thoughts of good and not of evil, toward them; forgiving their iniquities, rebuking and chastening them, but always readily receiving them again into His favor.   It was this which was indelibly impressed on the observant minds in Israel, that Jehovah was a God bent upon the redemption of His people, and that He was ever alongside of them, carrying forward into higher stages this redemptive work.   The Psalms and the Prophets are standing evidence that this was the impression made upon Israel — that God had actually made Himself known as the Redeemer of His people.

But all this revealing history, with the vary- *Revelation*
ing experience of God's people under His hand, *in Christ.*
and the various redemptive institutions which
kept alive the knowledge of God already won;
all *that* through which God made His presence
felt and His attitude known, prepared for and
culminated in the consummate revelation made
in Christ. Two aspects of this revelation manifest its perfectness, — its personality and its
redeeming efficacy.

(1) It is personal and thus perfect. In *Personal*
Christ, God manifests His personal attributes *and there-*
— His holiness, His love, His self-sacrifice — *fore perfect*
in personal, human actings. He brings Him-
self into intelligible connection with human
affairs. Only when Christ appeared could it
be said, " He that hath seen Me hath seen the
Father." Only then could men say, This that
we see in Jesus is the sympathy of God, the
devotedness and self-sacrifice, the forgiveness
and solicitude for the sinner that are in God.
Accordingly, He introduced the highest idea of
God men have ever cherished, — an idea introduced by His own year or two of public life
and by which now all other ideas are meas-

ured. Sometimes one feels as if in attributing
to God all good we were merely creating a God
out of our own fancies and ideals. But when
we turn to Christ we find that it is from His
historical figure we have borrowed our ideals.
In Christ we have all the God we seek. In
Him we have a personal revelation of a personal God. It required a Person fully to reveal God.

Redemp-
tively per-
fect.

(2) This revelation is also redemptively perfect. Christ revealed God not as abstractly
wise and holy and loving, but as expressing
and using all Divine virtue and resource with a
particular end in view, — that of redeeming us
from evil. And this has so been achieved in
Christ that it need not be undertaken over
again, nor need additions and supplements be
made to His work. When He said, "I have
finished the work thou gavest me to do," he
uttered a bare truth. In Him God has recon-
ciled the world unto Himself. God's thirst
for our salvation can never be more clearly expressed; nor shall we ever again see the power
of God unto salvation so put forth.

Method of
revelation.

4. We have to ask, What has been the method
of revelation? Our answer to this question depends upon our idea of God. If we believe in
God as immanent in the world and man, then

we shall necessarily believe that God reveals
Himself through human sensitiveness to the
Spiritual and inquiry after Him. If we believe
in God as merely transcendent, we shall think
of Him as moving man from without. In the
one case revelation will be internal and natural;
in the other it will be external and supernatural.

Belief in the immanence of God tends to *Immanence*
abolish the distinction between the natural and *of God.*
the supernatural. Everything is equally natural, or, if we prefer it, equally supernatural.
All nature is filled with the presence and power
of the living God. "The lily can as little
bloom without the forthputting of His energy
as the prophet can reveal Him or the saint grow
into His likeness." If, then, those who believe
in God's immanence maintain that all revelation is natural, this does not mean that it is not
under the direct control of God. It means
that revelation proceeds hand in hand with
human development, is driven forward by similar forces, and regulated by the same laws, all
of which are the manifestation and expression
of God.

The important point on which to fix atten- *Method is*
tion in our own day seems to be this : that *spiritual.*
whether we believe in the immanence of God
or think of Him as transcendent, we must bear

in mind that in any case He is spirit, and that
His operations are spiritual. When it is said
that He "spoke" to Moses and the prophets,
enjoining this or that institution, or communi-
cating this or that message, we are not to think
of any external intimation coming through the
bodily ear, but we are to understand that the
mind and spirit of the prophet were enabled to
perceive what was the mind of God. It was
through severe mental exercise that Paul attained his insight into Divine things and his
decisions on the difficult questions of practice
which were referred to him. As Sabatier says:
"When God wished to give the Decalogue to Israel, He did not write with His finger on tables
of stone; He raised up Moses, and from the
consciousness of Moses the Decalogue sprang.
In order that we might have the Epistle to
the Romans, there was no need to dictate it
to the Apostle; God had only to create the
powerful individuality of Saul of Tarsus, well
knowing that when once the tree was made,
the fruit would follow in due course." [1]

Instances of revelation.   In the thirteenth chapter of the book of
Acts we have a significant instance of reve-
lation. We there read that as certain Christian
teachers were praying, "the Holy Ghost said,

[1] "Outlines of Philosophy of Religion," p. 57.

Separate me Barnabas and Saul for the work whereunto I have called them." No reader of these words fancies that a voice audible to the bodily ear was heard uttering this commandment. Every reader understands that the Holy Ghost worked His will in a much more inward and effectual manner, speaking within the mind and spirit of those who sought His guidance. Neither can we suppose that without any previous expenditure of thought on the subject these men had this idea flashed into their mind as a bolt from the blue. It came as the result of their endeavor to discover what was the mind of God or, in other words, what was best in the circumstances to be done. They were inwardly convinced that the step they proposed was the mind of God. No more important step was ever taken in the history of the Church than the mission of Paul and Barnabas. And this step was taken on the safest, surest ground of inward revelation of the mind of Christ. They were convinced that they were fulfilling His will and seeing with His eyes. Here we have a key to the method of revelation. Men in sympathy with God understand His will, enter into His thought, recognize His judgments and His purposes, and so become organs of His revelation.

Criterion of revelation.

But if it is thus impossible to separate the thoughts of man from the revelation of God, it may be asked, How can any one certainly know what is from God and what is not from God? what is the Divine spirit informing the mind with true views of Divine things, and what is a lying spirit leading men astray? what is God making Himself and His will known, and what is human fancy and error? To such questioning it can only be replied that " for the individual prophet or apostle, himself no test of the genuineness of the revelations made to him could be superior to his own firm and clear conviction of such communion with God."

" Whoso has felt the spirit of the Highest
    Cannot confound, nor doubt Him, nor deny;
    Yea, with one voice, Oh! world, though thou deniest,
    Stand thou on that side, for on this am I."

And if it be asked whether the Church or community of godly people is bound to receive such communications on the word of the prophet, the answer is, No! the community has a responsibility as well as the prophet and must receive or reject his word according to its own consciousness of truth and of God in the message.

But the method of revelation will be more fully understood if we ask : —

5. Finally, what was God's purpose in re- *Purpose of*
vealing Himself to man? It may be said gen- *revelation.*
erally that God, being a God of love, sought to
communicate and impart of His own fulness to
all whom He had made in His image, capable
of holding fellowship with Him. But in considering particularly the revelation recorded in
the Bible we see that a more definite and particular purpose may be said to be in view. For
from first to last in the Bible man is represented
as needing redemption, deliverance from evil
and sin. Its opening scene is the fall of man,
and all God's revelation of Himself in Israel and
in Jesus Christ was a revelation in view of
man's sin. It was a manifestation of God as a
God of grace, as a Redeemer. And it was a
revelation which it concerned all men to know.
We may, therefore, reasonably conclude that
God's purpose was to bring the knowledge of
Himself as Redeemer to all men.

But to obtain this result it was necessary that *Recipients*
more should be done than merely that God *of revela-*
should manifest Himself in the history and *tion.*
institutions of Israel or even in the person and
life of Jesus Christ. It was needful that there
should be men fitted to recognize and appreciate
these manifestations. The initial and rudimentary intimations of God's presence were

made to all men. Not to the Jews alone, but
to all men has God manifested Himself as
a ruler who loves righteousness. But where
these preparatory lessons were not received,
higher lessons could not be given. In Israel
were found men fitted to understand what God
meant to teach. They were men whose spirit
was in sympathy with God. In other words,
inspiration was required to implement revelation. In order to utilize revelation there must
be men who have so much of God's spirit in
them as to discern, appreciate, and respond to
His manifestation in nature, in history, and in
Christ. And if this knowledge and appreciation of God's revelation are to be a permanent
possession of the race, it must be recorded in
writing.

Apparently, then, if revelation is to answer
its purpose, it must be made to those who can
understand it, and it must be recorded.

Here, then, emerge two points which call for
fuller discussion: (1) the progressiveness of
revelation and (2) its record in writing.

Revelation
progressive.   1. Revelation must be progressive because
it must accommodate itself to the condition of
those to whom it is made. It used to be one
of the stock difficulties of the Deists, Why did
not God reveal Himself in Christ at first?

Why did He not follow up the fall with the immediate manifestation of His grace? And in our own day it is commonly objected to the Old Testament that its morality is imperfect — a difficulty as old as the second century, when so many of the Gnostic sects were stumbled by what they found in the Old Testament and declared that it was a different God who is there represented. All such difficulties are overcome as soon as it is recognized that by the nature of the case God was compelled to accommodate Himself to the condition of those with whom He had to do. It was impossible that in the childhood of the race such a knowledge of God could be received as was possible in its maturity.

When Plotinus said, "He must become godlike who desires to see God," he uttered the principle which lies at the root of the matter. "Moral affinity is an essential of personal intimacy. A man cannot understand a character with which his own has no accord." We cannot make ourselves understood by those who are utterly unlike ourselves, neither can God. A loving and unselfish man, who goes among persons hardened by vice and who have never known love, is sure at first to be misunderstood, and it is only by degrees he can make his character known. At first he will be sus-

Accommodation to recipients.

pected, misjudged. And it has been only in proportion as men have become capable of appreciating the higher and diviner qualities of character that God has been able to disclose Himself more and more fully to the race. The love of God could not be understood until His righteousness and holiness were understood. It was useless for Christ to die until the heart and conscience of men had firmly grasped holiness and righteousness as essential to Divinity — then only could His self-sacrificing love be fully appreciated and intelligently estimated.

Morality of Old Testament

So, too, with the morality of the Old Testament. By slow degrees morality had to be cleansed and heightened, and if we wish to ascertain whether it is a Divinely guided process which the Old Testament records, we must ask, not what the early stages were, but what the whole process resulted in. The circumstance that men in some sense inspired, and who at any rate were the organs of revelation, as Abraham and David, were guilty of lying and other iniquities, testifies to the truth of the record and reflects no discredit on the revelation. In so far as the Divine accommodation adapted itself to the imperfectly moral, *with the result of raising them to a higher level*, that procedure is justified.

This point is so constantly misunderstood *and infer-ences there-from.* that a word or two more may be given to it. There are in the Old Testament not only immoralities recorded, as there must be in any full and true history, but there are actions recorded which seem to have the Divine sanction and yet are condemned by the New Testament code. The practice of slavery and polygamy, the slaughter of the Canaanites and the priests of Baal, the destruction of innocent children along with their guilty parents, the ferocious and vindictive expressions in many of the Psalms addressed to God, — these frequently stumble readers of the Bible.

Regarding these things the argument of scep- *Sceptical argument.* tics is a brief one : This book professes to be Divine, but it represents God as approving of immoral actions and, therefore, it cannot be Divine. Its claim is false, and we must disregard it.

This argument was perhaps justified by the *Its fallacy.* claims which used to be made for the Bible and by the manner in which these claims were urged ; but the argument has no relevancy against the real claim of the Old Testament and the just and true view of God's method of evealing Himself. The Old Testament is a aithful record of a race which was being

trained to know God and to love righteousness,
and it shows us the steps in their progress.
The leading men of this race were sincere and
devoted servants of Jehovah and were in true
communion with Him, but they had not a perfect knowledge of Him.   They were gradually
advancing toward that perfect knowledge which
came only with Christ.   They were able to
understand only so much of the Divine nature
as they had grown up to, as a child cannot
understand the whole of his father's character
and ways.   And these imperfections in the
knowledge of God, the Bible, being a true
and faithful record, freely recounts ; briefly
showing us how the best men among the Jews
misunderstood God, but how, by adhering to
His law and seeking to hold fellowship with
Him, they gradually eliminated from their
knowledge of Him all that was crude and un-
worthy.   And it is not the imperfections and
mistakes which disfigure the earlier parts of
this growth which should arrest our attention,
but the sure and grand progress that at last
left behind all these imperfections and justified
the training hand and spirit of God.   To look
upon the Old Testament as depicting a final
stage in knowledge or righteousness, and not
as a preparation, is a fatal error ; to look upon

each part of God's revelation by itself and judge it in separation from what goes before and after, is a fatal error. If we would have clear views, either of revelation or of the Old Testament, we must above all bear in mind that revelation was a growing light from dawn to perfect day, and that though some in the gray dawn trusted God and served Him as faithfully as their successors, it was not possible that they should know Him as well.

The summary argument of the sceptic, there- *True con-* fore, falls to the ground when it meets the only *ception of* *Old Testa-* true idea of the Old Testament. The sceptic *ment.* who coarsely selects from the Old Testament all that shocks the modern conscience and thrusts all these crudities in the Christian's face, saying, "That is your God — a God who approves slavery and vengeance," and the devout reader who wishes these things were out of the book altogether, alike misconceive the real state of the case. God revealed Himself to men feature by feature as they were able to receive it. He did not lift the Jewish people at once and miraculously to the stage they were at length to reach. He did not supernaturally impart to the race at one flash the knowledge of Himself which He meant to give them by guiding their national history, by teaching their

best men to reflect upon that history and strive
to advance it. He revealed Himself to them
through their national life, through His dealings with them in their times of rebellion and
repentance. He was in no hurry to remove
misconceptions; they could only see in Him
what they had grown up to be able to see; and
serving Him according to their present knowledge was the only method of growing to know
more. The circumstance, therefore, that even
men like Elijah had not as yet the conception
of God that Christ has given us, and served
Him in ways that our conscience cannot
approve, is only another proof that the Old
Testament is a true and helpful account of the
actual process by which God revealed Himself
to man.

Christ the
criterion of
revelation.

It will, however, be said: If this is so, if the
Old Testament records the misconceptions of
good men as well as their contributions to the
permanent knowledge of God, are we not liable
to mistake the one for the other? If God is
not in some particulars what some of these men
thought Him, how are we to know as we read
the Old Testament what to receive and what
to reject? The person and teaching of Christ
are our test. In His perfect revelation of the
Father we have the criterion by which all

that is imperfect is judged. By the finished
product we judge each part of the process
which prepared for it. If you read the history of the steam engine, or of engraving, or
of electricity, or of astronomy, or any science,
you find that discovery has gone forward step
by step, and that brilliant ideas were often
accompanied by mistakes which for a time kept
back the result. And in tracing out the long
history of any discovery, it is not the mistakes
that chiefly engage the historian's attention,
but the continuous thread of progress that
connects the earliest thinker with the latest.
And no modern astronomer is misled by the
mistaken ideas regarding the motion of the
sun which were current in ancient times ; nor
is the engineer who possesses the actual working machine perplexed by the false expectations of early investigators into the power of
steam. And no sane person would think of
pouring scorn upon those who in bygone centuries worked at any science, but did so with
many misapprehensions of the truth. They,
with all their mistakes and strivings, were the
necessary antecedents to our knowledge. In
the discovery of God there is indeed a difference. God revealed Himself, and did not leave
man to his natural powers of discovery; but on

the other hand God could only discover to man
what he was fit to understand, and this understanding was regulated by the real historical
growth of the human mind.   To look back
with contempt, then, on the thoughts and actions of Old Testament saints is a kind of
spiritual parricide ; it is to forget the rock
from which we are hewn; it is to despise the
great pioneers who have made our knowledge
possible.

Revelation,
why re-
corded.

2. God's purpose in revealing Himself being
to redeem mankind, it was, if not necessary, yet
most desirable that the revelation should be
recorded.

Bishop Butler has indeed said that " we
are not in any sort able to judge whether it
were to have been expected that the revelation should have been committed to writing;
or left to be handed down, and consequently
corrupted by verbal tradition, and at length
sunk under it, if mankind so pleased, and
during such time as they are permitted, in the
degree they evidently are, to act as they will.
But it may be said, ' That a revelation in some
of the above-mentioned circumstances, one, for
instance, which was not committed to writing,
and thus secured against danger of corruption,
would not have answered its purpose.'   I ask,

what purpose? It would not have answered
all the purposes which it has now answered,
and in the same degree; but it would have
answered others or the same in different
degrees. And which of these were the purposes of God, and best fell in with His general
government, we could not at all have determined beforehand." This is a most useful
corrective to our readiness to presume that
such and such must have been God's purposes,
as well as a reminder that revelation is one
thing, the recording of it another, and that it
is quite conceivable that there might have been
a revelation without any written record of it.
Certainly a large part of God's revelation of
Himself has been lost. Much of His revelation in nature is not yet understood; His
revelation in history has been only partially
recognized; even His revelation in Christ is
not fully recorded. But although beforehand
it might have been presumptuous to predict
what would happen, yet now that we find so
full a record of God's revelation actually made,
it is very easy to recognize the immense advantage of this procedure. This is nowhere better
stated than in the Westminster Confession.
" Although the light of nature, and the works
of creation and providence, do so far manifest

the goodness, wisdom, and power of God, as to leave men inexcusable, yet they are not sufficient to give that knowledge of God and of His will which is necessary unto salvation; therefore it pleased the Lord at sundry times and in divers manners to reveal Himself and to declare that His will unto His Church; and afterwards for the better preserving and propagating of the truth, and for the more sure establishment and comfort of the Church against the corruption of the flesh and the malice of Satan and of the world, to commit the same wholly unto writing; which maketh the holy Scripture to be most necessary; those former ways of God's revealing His will unto His people being now ceased." To the same effect says Rothe: "We must not forget that the main point in revelation is not that it shall produce an effect on the immediate sphere in which it is operative, but that the facts in which it consists shall be abidingly present for man in his intellectual horizon, as an essential *datum* in the complex of his perceptions and experiences. It seeks to introduce certain facts as elements of the human world, which this world could not have produced of itself."

Need of written records.

It may therefore be said that it is impossible for us to see how the revelation could have ac-

complished its ends had it not been committed
to writing: for, first, it is even difficult to understand how the revelation could have been
completed without the aid of writing. The
revelation was historical, extending over long
periods of time. "One generation must tell to
another the truths revealed and the redemptive
deeds accomplished by God." The prophets
built upon the antecedent Law and on the previous history of the people. The New Testament writers were guided and aided by their
knowledge of the Old Testament. And it is
not apparent that in any other way than by
means of written records the continuity and progressiveness of the revelation could have been
maintained. As Professor Ladd says: "Biblical revelation is not spasmodic; it is historical. Memory is as necessary to the growth of
the race as of the individual. It belongs to
the very idea of an historical revelation that
there should be an accumulated store of Divine
Communications."

Again, it is the written record which pre-
serves incorrupt and propagates through all
ages and all tongues the knowledge of God as
Redeemer which He has communicated. If
any one wishes to know what God is in His
relation to man, if it be desired to know what

Christianity is, or what are the facts on which
Christianity is based and the doctrines it de-
livers, or if it be in dispute what men ought to
believe, it is to the Bible appeal must be made.
And therefore the Bible may itself legitimately,
if loosely, be called the revelation.

Summary.   *Conclusion.*—From all this, then, it will be
gathered that God has revealed Himself especially in His redemptive energy, that we see
most of God and of all that is essential to His
character and purposes in His approaches to man
and education of man in order to restore him to
Himself and to free him absolutely from all
evil.   In the Bible we have the written history
of this approach of God to man, the record of
His revelation of His gracious and saving purposes and work.   To think of it as a convenient collection or summary of doctrines, a
text-book in theological knowledge, is entirely
to misconceive it.   "If we get out of it a system
of truth as to God and His relations to man, we
must do it as an astronomer gets a system of
astronomy from the heavenly bodies" (or as an
embryologist gathers his completed information
from watching the natural growth of the em-
bryo).   God has revealed Himself, and the leading facts of this revelation are recorded for us
in the Bible, and from these facts we can gather

what God wishes us to know about Him and how He wishes us to think of Him. But the Bible must not be thought of as "a collection of truths formulated in propositions which God from time to time whispered in the ear to be communicated to the world as the unchanging formulas of thought and life for all time." [1]

Here, also, we get the idea of inspiration, for this revelation of God can only be understood and appreciated by those who have His spirit — inspired men must be there to receive the revelation. Inspiration is the complement of revelation — as sight is the complement of the external world; it is that in man which perceives, appreciates, accepts, and in certain cases records the revelation of God. There may be revelation by God where there is no inspired man to observe and respond to it as there are parts of the external world the eye has never seen. But the essential elements in revelation have been understood and interpreted by men. Much revelation has been made which there were no inspired men to receive; and much revelation has been perceived by inspired men which has not been recorded. In the Bible we have that selected revelation which inspired men have accepted and seen fit to record.

[1] Harris, p. 458.

IV

INSPIRATION

IV

INSPIRATION

THREE things, then, should be held distinct in our minds: God's revelation of Himself, human apprehension of this revelation, and the record in our Bible of this revelation as apprehended. It is not indeed conceivable that such a revelation of God as was made in Christ should have failed to find appreciative minds; and, as during a long period of the world's history men had been accustomed to put in writing what had impressed them, it was natural that the further step of recording a recognized revelation should be taken. But by holding these three processes distinct in our mind we gain a clearer apprehension of the nature and place of the Bible. Prior to the existence of the Bible, God manifested Himself savingly to men; but it is equally true that it is through the Bible God now makes Himself and His redemption apprehensible by men. God revealed Himself in Christ and saved the world in Christ before there was any New Testament; but the benefit

Revelation and its record.

101

of that revelation is permanently conveyed to
the world through the Gospels and the epistles.
Accordingly, the Scriptures have been described
as " the mode by which God as He is in Christ
lives for the faith of the Church and before
the mind of the world.   They as it were so
impersonate, immortalize, and universalize the
consciousness of Christ that it can exercise
everywhere and always its creative and normative functions."   Roughly, therefore, the Bible
is called the revelation of God because it brings
before us in a written record what God has
done to make Himself known, and what God-
inspired men have seen in that revelation and
have thought of God.[1]   The human qualifica-
tion for understanding and recording revelation
requires fuller treatment.   It is called *Inspi-*
ration, which is the word used to translate
Inspiration.   θεοπνευστία.   This quality is claimed for Scrip-

[1] Obviously, this involves that in order to appreciate and
use the Bible the reader of it must himself have the same
spirit which enabled its writers to understand the revelation
of God and to record it.   The Bible is a record, but it is not
a dead record of dead persons and events, but a record inspired by the living Spirit who uses it to speak to men now.
It is more than a phonograph which has mechanically stored
up for ages the words and tones of the original speaker.   It
is the medium through which the living God now makes
Himself heard and known.   But to find in it the Spirit of
God the reader must himself have that Spirit.

ture and for the writers of it : (1) On the grounds already stated that the presence of the Divine Spirit is requisite to enable a man to recognize God's revelation. Spiritual things are spiritually discerned. Accordingly, our Lord promised nothing more emphatically and explicitly than the coming of this Spirit of truth that His people might recognize what God had revealed in Him. And (2) while the writers of Scripture do not individually claim this inspiration, but rest their claims to credence rather upon other qualifications, yet in the New Testament inspiration is claimed for the Old. In 2 Tim. iii. 16, however we construe the words, inspiration is claimed for Scripture; and in 2 Pet. i. 21 we have the statement that prophecy was not the product of human will, but men from God spake being carried (φερόμενοι) or borne along by the Holy Spirit. Paul, too, in 1 Cor. xiv. 37, says, " If any man thinks he is a prophet or spiritual, let him acknowledge that what I write is of the Lord." And when in another part of the same epistle (vii. 40) he says, " I think (δοκῶ) that I have the spirit of God," the modesty of the claim only gives us additional certification of its truth. And if other writers whose books appear in Scripture make no such claim, this by no means involves that they did not possess inspiration.

Various definitions.

But when we attempt to advance from the simple affirmation that Scripture is inspired to the inquiry, What is inspiration? we find ourselves beset with various contradictory opinions. Every gradation of opinion has found advocates from the lowest to the highest; from the idea that the writers of Scripture were inspired in the same sense as Milton or Bunyan or Beethoven was inspired, to the belief that inspiration means that every word in the Bible is as fully the word of God as if no human instrumentality had intervened.

A priori conception inadmissible.

Much injustice has been done to the Bible, and much harm has resulted to faith, by allowing *a priori* conceptions of inspiration and its effects to rule. It has been argued that if God is pleased to make known His will to men, this revelation must be accomplished in such and such a manner. It will be clear and unambiguous in meaning; it will be unadulterated by any alloy of human error, and so forth. Thus it was argued that the Hebrew vowel-points must have been inspired, for otherwise the reading would have been uncertain, and God could not leave uncertainty in His word. Similarly, it was argued that God could allow

no grammatical errors, no barbarous construc-
tions, no faultiness of style in His word. Tex-
tual criticism was frowned upon because it was
supposed that God could not leave His word to
the mercy of the ordinary accidents affecting
secular literature. All these preconceptions
have been found to be erroneous and have lent
emphasis to the warning pronounced by Bishop
Butler: " We are in no sense judges beforehand
by what methods and in what proportion it
were to be expected that this supernatural
light and instruction should be afforded us.
The only question concerning the authority of
Scripture is whether it be what it claims to be,
not whether it be a book of such sort and so
promulgated as weak men are apt to fancy a
book containing a Divine revelation should be.
And therefore neither obscurity, nor seeming
inaccuracy of style, nor various readings, nor
early disputes about the authors, nor any other
things of the like kind, though they had been
much more considerable than they are, could
overthrow the authority of Scripture, unless
the prophets, apostles, or our Lord had promised that the Book containing the Divine revelation should be secure from these things."

It is, then, only from the Bible itself we can
learn what an inspired book is. We may find

*Inspiration
to be learned
from Bible
itself.*

many unexpected peculiarities in the Bible, but these will not dismay us, if we have not gone to it with a preconceived theory of what it *ought* to be and of what inspiration *must* accomplish. The Bible must not be forced into conformity with our Procrustean theory of inspiration; but we must allow our theory to be formed by the Bible. If we should find on examination that much of what is human enters into the Bible, we must expand our theory to include this. If we should find discrepancies or inaccuracies, these must help us to our true theory.

In Professor Bowne's small but excellent book on the "Christian Revelation," he very truly says: "The presence of inspiration is discernible in the product, but the meaning and measure of inspiration cannot be decided by abstract reflection, but only by the outcome. What inspiration is, must be learned from what it does. We must not determine the character of the books from the inspiration, but must rather determine the nature of the inspiration from the books" (pp. 44–45).

Problem of inspiration. The problem in regard to inspiration is, to adjust truly the Divine and the human factors. The various theories which have been framed and held differ from one another regarding the proportion which the human element in the process and in the result bears to the Divine. According as greater or less predominance is ascribed to the Divine influence we have the following theories : —

1. That which has been known as the mechanical or dictation theory. It is the theory of complete possession, in which the Divine factor is at its maximum, the human at its minimum. What is human is suppressed; the indwelling God uses the human organs irrespective of the human will. The man is the mere mouthpiece of the god, uttering words he need not know the meaning of, thoughts which no free process of his own faculties has reached. He is the organ of a mind and will not his own. *Mechanical theory.*

This view has always been popular outside of Christianity. Among heathen people the very sign of a man's being possessed by a god is that he loses self-control. Paul's rule that the spirit of the prophet is subject to the prophet was incomprehensible to them. The less command the prophet had over himself the more surely was he inspired. Accordingly, this state of frenzy was artificially produced by inhaling fumes or by violent dancings and contortions, such as are still practised in Africa and the East. Similarly, persons in a state of *This a heathen theory.*

trance can see what is invisible to them when in possession of their faculties, and dreams are supposed to be intimations of the Divine will. This view of inspiration is announced not only as the superstition of the heathen populace, but by their authoritative exponents of belief. Plato, for example, in the "Timæus" (71) says, "God has given the art of divination, not to the wisdom, but to the foolishness of man. No man, when in his wits, attains prophetic truth and inspiration; but when he receives the inspired word, either his intelligence is enthralled in sleep, or he is demented by some distemper or possession." And in the "Phædrus" (244) he gives an account of four forms of madness, — prophecy, inspiration, poetry, love, and shows that the self-possessed man cannot be the subject of these inspirations.

ἔκφρων was the word commonly used to express the human side of the condition most receptive of Divine communications. Thus in Plato's "Ion," 534, occurs the expression ἔνθεός τε καὶ ἔκφρων, and in Plutarch's "Themistocles," c. XXVI., 2, a certain tutor Olbios suddenly becomes inspired, ἔκφρων γενόμενος καὶ θεοφόρητος. In the sixth "Æneid" Virgil represents the priestess as striving to shake off the god and struggling against his influence till she is gradually subdued.

This theory, then, proceeds upon the idea that the less the ordinary human faculties are in operation, the fuller is the Divine inspiration. It is supposed that God finds freer expression for Himself, not through the fuller exercise of the human mind and spirit, but through their suppression. Hence the relation of the inspiring God to the inspired man was often pictured by that of a player to the lyre or harp on which he played, or of a writer to the pen with which he wrote. The man was a mechanical instrument, and into the work accomplished his own thought, feeling, and will did not enter. The result was purely Divine; every word uttered was the word of God. *Human faculty suppressed.*

Only in some disguised form can this theory now be held, although certainly it was common until quite recently, and it has whatever prestige antiquity can give it. Some of the fathers, especially Athenagoras, used the figure of the lyre and the plectrum in a manner which at least lays them open to the suspicion of holding this mechanical theory. Athenagoras, speaking of the prophets, says, that " while entranced and *deprived of their natural powers of reason* by the influence of the Divine Spirit, they uttered that which was wrought in them, the spirit using them as its instruments, as a flute- *Popularity of this theory.*

player might blow a flute." Philo, with all his intelligence and knowledge, believed that inspiration was a kind of ecstasy, and that inspired men were mere voices uttering not what they had themselves felt and thought, but God's words.[1]

*Jewish be-
lief.*

Hence to the Jews every word and letter of the Scriptures was sacred. When Moses went up into the Mount he found Jehovah making the ornamental letters in the book of the Law. Accordingly, they numbered the words and the letters of every book, and found a mystery full of significance in the most external and casual features of the sacred book.

*Outcome of
this theory.*

In the second century, Montanism gave an impulse to this mechanical view and was explicitly opposed by Miltiades in a treatise entitled περὶ τοῦ μὴ δεῖν προφήτην ἐν ἐκστάσει λαλεῖν, *i.e. That the prophet ought not to speak in ecstasy.* But the hold which this theory took even upon Christendom is perhaps best

---

[1] Philo (" Quis Rer. Div. Haeres," c. 53, p. 511, Mangey, Vol. I.) says that so long as we are masters of ourselves, we are not possessed by any extraneous influence ; but when our own mind ceases to shine, inspiration and madness lay hold of us. " For the understanding that dwells in us is ousted on the arrival of the Divine Spirit, but is restored to its own dwelling when that Spirit departs, for it is unlawful that mortal dwell with immortal."

illustrated by the fact that it found expression
in the post-reformation "Formula Consensus
Helvetici," in which occurs this clause: Hebra-
icus V. T. codex, tum quoad consonas, tum
quoad vocalia, sive puncta ipsa, seu punctorum
saltem potestatem, et tum quoad res, tum quoad
verba θεοπνευστός.

A theory of which this is the legitimate logi- *This theory
cal outcome does not cover the facts of Scrip- untenable.*
ture, and therefore becomes untenable. The
account which Luke gives us of his preparation
for writing his Gospel shows that he was not a
mere mouthpiece of another's thoughts. If
the penitential wailings and joyful thanksgiv-
ings and ascriptions of praise which we find in
the Psalms are not the fruit of human sorrow
and of human thought and experience, they at
once become vapid and false. It is inconceivable, and contrary to all we know of the manner of God's working, that He should have
used men in this merely mechanical way.

And the supposed *result* of this supposed *Its supposed
process is as incongruous with God's usual result.*
methods. The supposed result is a Bible in
which every word is as truly the word of God
as if He spoke it directly to ourselves apart
from all human intervention. There cannot be
the faintest infusion of error. Every histori-

cal, scientific, or chronological statement is exactly true. It is, however, needless to follow this theory into all its difficulties and inconsistencies. It makes demands that cannot be satisfied. It requires that we have a Bible of which we are sure that each book is divinely inspired in this absolutely inerrant sense; that no book has been admitted which is not thus authorized. It demands, also, that we have a solution for all discrepancies in the several books. If such a Bible was necessary, then steps would have been taken to secure it to us. But in point of fact we have a Bible which we know does not in every particular tally with that which at first was received. Manuscripts have been corrupted, translations are inexact; but it is with these that the Christian people have practically to do. So that the result of this theory of infallibility is not, after all, to put in our hands an infallible Bible, but actually to rob us of it. It is only the original autographs which can claim such an infallibility; and these are forever beyond our reach. Had verbal accuracy been required for our saving use of the Bible, it would have been secured. It has not been secured, therefore it was not required.

If it were requisite that we should know the

very words originally written, then were we *Divergence* *of the text.* hopelessly shut out from the benefit of God's word. For the text used by the Jews of the centuries immediately preceding the Christian era is not the Hebrew text we now use. The text they used can be discovered from the LXX [1]; but the LXX is, to a considerable extent, different from our Bible. Not only are incidents in the life of David which we read in our text omitted from the LXX, but in a prophet so important as Jeremiah about one-eighth of what we find in the Hebrew is omitted from the Greek, while the arrangement of the material widely differs. Who can tell us which of these texts, the Hebrew we now use or the Hebrew used by the LXX, is nearer the original? No one can certainly say.

There are two facts of Scripture which are incompatible with the theory of verbal inspiration.

(1) The first of these is the manner in which *Quotations* *of Old Tes-* quotations from the Old Testament are made *tament in* in the New. Of such quotations there are *the New.* 275.[2]

---

[1] That is, the Septuagint translation of the Old Testament into Greek.

[2] See Toy's "Quotations from Old Testament."

Of these there are only 53 in which the
Hebrew, the LXX, and the New Testament
agree; that is, in which the LXX has
correctly rendered the Hebrew and been
correctly quoted by the New Testament
writer 53

There are 10 interesting passages in which the
LXX has been corrected and brought into
harmony with the Hebrew . . . 10

There are 37 passages in which the faulty rendering of the LXX has been accepted in the
New Testament quotation . . . 37

There are 76 passages in which the correct
version of the LXX has been altered into
a rendering which does not agree with the
original 76

And there are 99 passages in which the New
Testament quotation differs both from the
Hebrew and from the LXX . . 99

Now, on any explanation of this style of
quoting, it would certainly seem as if the New
Testament writers thought much more of the
sense of the sacred Scriptures than of the language. No doubt the language may in some
cases be so involved with the thought that
regard must be had to the actual wording of
the utterance. A case in point is the argu-

ment founded by Paul on the use of a singular instead of a plural. But commonly one form of words may express a thought almost as adequately as another; and as the above statistics prove, the New Testament writers set no special store by the exact words in which the Old Testament writers expressed themselves.

It may be fancied that if this is the practice of the New Testament writers, it runs counter to the explicit affirmation of Christ that not a jot or tittle of the law should pass away till all be fulfilled. But it is only by reckless carelessness that these words can be applied to the words of Scripture at all. What our Lord means is, as the context shows, that nothing which God has ordained in the law or promised in the prophets shall pass away till it has been fulfilled in Him. Immediately upon saying this He proceeds to repeal commandments of the law, substituting for them commandments of His own, showing that what He has in view is not Scripture as Scripture, and that the fulfilment He thinks of is absorption in Himself.

(2) The second fact of Scripture which appears to be incompatible with the idea of verbal inspiration is the fact that those who record the sayings of our Lord greatly differ in their reports. One would expect that here, if any.

Report of our Lord's words not literally exact.

where, sacredness would attach to the very
letter and precise language used. But it is
not so. Even in reporting the Lord's Prayer
the evangelists differ; and in His ordinary
sayings and conversations we congratulate
ourselves if the sense is the same in the
different Gospels and scarcely expect to find
absolute identity of language. But if inspiration involved perfect accuracy of language,
no such phenomena as the Gospels present
would appear.

Paul not an advocate of verbal inspiration.　There is indeed a statement made by Paul
which to the superficial reader might seem to
indicate that he believed himself to be taught
by the Holy Ghost *the very words* in which he
was to declare Christian truth. In 1 Cor.
ii., speaking of the things God had revealed
through His Spirit, he says, "Which things
also we speak not in the words which man's
wisdom teacheth, but which the Holy Ghost
teacheth." But Paul's intention is to contrast
two methods of teaching, two styles of language, — the worldly and the spiritual, — and to
affirm that the style he adopts was that which
the Holy Ghost taught him. He meant to
justify his use of a certain *kind* of language
and a certain *style* of teaching. The Spirit of
the world adopts one method of insinuating

knowledge into the mind; the Spirit of God
uses another method.

The idea of verbal inspiration has arisen
from the notion that the Spirit of God inserts
or puts into the mind of the inspired man a
truth, as it were ready-made, and not in any
necessary connection with the previous contents of the inspired mind or its normal action. In this case, no doubt, the thought would
naturally be given in a definite form of words.
But everything in the Bible discourages this
idea. The impact of the Spirit's influence occurs at a point more remote from the result
than verbal inspiration presumes. It is the
man who is inspired. It is not that one inspired thought is magically communicated to
him in the form in which he is to declare it to
his fellows. But the man himself is inspired,
so that he with all his natural powers and idiosyncrasies becomes the organ of the Spirit. The
elevating, refining, spiritual influence of inspiration may be compared in its mode of action to
the influence of some new passion, say, maternal
love, in the subject of it. It seizes upon the
whole person and uses all the faculties for
its purposes. Inspiration, therefore, does not
lift the inspired person out of all his limitations, but uses him as he is, and all his facul-

Verbal inspiration based on error.

ties as they are for the fulfilment of a Divine purpose.

2. Abandoning, then, this theory of possession as untenable, we find a proposed relief from its inconsistencies in the theory that the Divine energy did not annihilate the human coöperation. The Divine influence was dominant, but not overpowering. Modifications of the theory of possession are probably due to the Jewish Rabbis. They differentiated the Law, the Prophets, and the Kethubim. For the inspiration of the Kethubim, or Hagiographa, they considered that only a small degree of inspiration was needed, a higher degree for the prophetic writings and the highest for the Law. The schoolmen followed them and some distinguish four degrees of influence: *superintendence*, which saved from positive error; *elevation*, which imparted loftiness to the thought; *direction*, which prompted the writer what to insert and what to omit; and *suggestion*, which inspired both thoughts and words.[1] Without definitely holding these various degrees or modes of the Divine influence, many have thought that difficulties would be escaped and the accuracy of Scripture sufficiently guaran-

---

[1] See *Jewish Encyclopedia*, art. "Inspiration"; also, Farrar's art. on "Inspiration" in *Theological Educator*.

teed if it were held that God inspired the
thoughts but not the words; that the truths
are communicated by the Holy Spirit, but the
form, the words and phrases in which they are
delivered, are due to the writer's own individuality. Plutarch has an interesting paper on
the Pythian responses in which the question is
discussed, why the oracles are not always given
in perfect form if they are Divine. And his
answer is twofold: (1) that the Pythia is not
less the organ of the god because she does not
clothe herself in purple robes and sprinkle herself with perfumes when she goes down into
the cave; the Passionless and the Pure does
not accord with what is pleasant to the senses;
and (2) that while the god supplies the inspiration, the verses in which the will of the god
is uttered are the productions of each of the
prophetesses in turn. "If she were obliged to
write down, and not to utter, the responses, we
should not, I suppose, believe the hand-writing
to be the god's, and to find fault with it, because
it is inferior in point of caligraphy to the im-
perial rescripts; for neither is the old woman's
voice, nor her diction, nor her metre the god's;
but it is the god alone who presents the visions
to this woman and kindles light in her soul regarding the future; for this is the inspiration."

*The dy-
namic
theory.*

This theory is known as the *dynamic*, and may roughly be said to embrace all theories which hold that the truths uttered in Scripture are Divine, while the imperfections and weaknesses are human.   Classical expression is given to this theory in the words of Augustine, who says that the writer is "inspiratus a Deo, sed tamen homo."   But not to mention that such a severance of the Divine and human in inspiration is impossible, this theory has been found to introduce confusion into the subject.

*Roman
Catholic
theory.*

To illustrate the working of this theory, let us take the statement of it by a Roman Catholic authority.[1]   "The only proper monotheistic idea of inspiration is that an All-wise and Almighty God chose and moved His instruments so that their action exactly corresponded to His will, and did not try to play lyre-music on flutes and harp-music on trumpets.   Further, that He used them as men preserving their human faculties, and that they knew and understood what they were saying and had said, though they need not, therefore, have known all the ultimate deductions from it, any more than a teacher of arithmetic need know the differential calculus."   This explanation promises well; but when this same writer goes on to declare that

[1] Tablet, May 5, 1894.

the words are the words of God, and that therefore all error is excluded, we see that this theory
with all its professions is as mechanical as the
dictation or possession theory. The papal en-
cyclical on the subject, issued by Pope Leo
XIII., declares that "those who maintain that
an error is possible in any genuine passage of
the sacred writings pervert the Catholic notion
of inspiration, and make God the Author of such
error." This theory does not satisfy the facts
of Scripture, and must therefore be pronounced
incompetent.

The only form in which the dynamic theory
can be admitted is that which has sometimes
been called the "essential" theory ; that is, the
theory that holds that the writers were so inspired as to secure accuracy in all matters of
conduct and doctrine, while it declines to pledge
itself to the perfect accuracy of the writers in
non-essentials, or subsidiary particulars. This
theory was held by Erasmus, Grotius, Baxter,
Paley, Döllinger, and the great mass of German
theologians. It recognizes that God had a purpose to accomplish by the Scriptures, and that
only such inspiration was required as is sufficient for the attainment of this purpose. Men
were employed as instruments in carrying out
this purpose, but they were so employed that

*The "essen-
tial" the-
ory.*

it was with their own free will, and using such means and material as they had, that they fulfilled God's purpose. His purpose was laid on human lines and was accomplished through the free working of human instruments.

Its inadequacy. Those who hold this theory view with perfect equanimity the investigations of criticism. If errors in history or science be discovered, or if discrepancies in the Gospels be pointed out, they say with Coleridge, " Perhaps they can be explained, perhaps they cannot, who cares a straw whether they can or no?" But while this theory is to be commended for its candor in endeavoring to recognize the facts of Scripture and to account for them, it cannot claim to bring us much nearer any understanding of inspiration itself. It does not explain, or even attempt to explain, how writers should be possessed of supernatural knowledge while inditing one sentence and be dropped to a much lower level in the next. It does not give us the psychology of that state of mind which can infallibly pronounce on matters of doctrine, while it is all astray on the simpler facts of history. It makes no attempt to analyze the relation subsisting between the Divine mind and the human, which produces such results. In short, it is rather a statement of the facts which Scripture presents than a theory accounting for the facts. It declares that Scripture is an infallible authority in essentials, but in non-essentials merely human ; but how we are to distinguish between these two elements in Scripture, or how we are to think of the state of mind of the writers, it does not explain.

We are left, then, without any sufficient theory, and we are often told that if not impossible, it is at least not safe, to define inspiration or form a theory on so obscure a subject.[1] But without professing to define inspiration it seems safe to affirm one or two elements which enter into it, and must be included in any definition.

What it is safe to affirm regarding inspiration.

1. The first affirmation which may safely be made regarding inspiration is that it signifies the presence and influence of the Divine Spirit. The Spirit of God may truly be said to be present and energetic everywhere. But the same result of His presence is not everywhere apparent. Infinitely various are human life and human need ; infinitely various also is the work

That it implies perception of revelation.

[1] Professor Wood proposes, as a tentative definition, the following : " Biblical inspiration is the personal influence of God which so guided all who took part in producing the Bible that they made a body of literature unique in religious value, and, so far as we now see, final in religious teaching." (See " A Tenable Theory of Inspiration," a lecture which cannot be too strongly recommended.)

of the Divine Spirit. Under the Old Testa
ment inspiration was claimed for those who, like
Bezaleel and Samson, by extraordinary powers
fulfilled in one direction or another the will of
God for His people. The writers of Scripture
are designated "inspired," not as if they alone
possessed the Spirit of God, but because in
them that spirit is working as the Spirit of
Christ toward this special end of perceiving
God in Christ and making Him permanently
known. All Christians possess the Spirit of
Christ and are, by Him, being led into a full
knowledge of the truth that is in Christ, to a
full perception of that whole revelation of God
which is made in Christ; and when some of
their number are *characterized* as "inspired,"
this means that these persons are distinguished
above their fellow-Christians by a special readiness and capacity to perceive the meaning of
Christ as the revelation of God and to make
known what they see.[1]

[1] "Inspiration is a personal term. It means the breathing in by one person of a power from another. It is,
broadly speaking, another term for personal influence, and
is usually kept for its higher, more uplifting phases. . . .
Divine inspiration is the influence of the Divine person upon
the human — of God upon man. . . . Biblical inspiration
is a species of inspiration in general. It is the influence of
God which resulted in the production of the Bible." (Professor Wood's "Tenable Theory," pp. 9, 10, 16.)

2. Inspiration stands in a vital relation to character. The Spirit of truth, promised to the disciples, was the Spirit of holiness. It was those who were most in sympathy with the purposes of God, and who were most imbued with the Spirit of holiness, who were best prepared to see and recount His revelations. The man who gave himself up to God, and who was emptied of self-seeking and of worldly ways of looking at things, was best fitted to understand what God sought to disclose to men. Such a man became the purest possible medium of the Spirit. What he sees, he sees clearly and truly, having no interest to see anything different from what God actually makes known. And what he sees, he utters authoritatively, knowing that it is not his own will, but the will of God he is declaring. The inspired man might not see the facts of history any more clearly than the uninspired; but he saw God in history where the uninspired only saw human passions.

That it implies godliness.

Inspiration, then, is primarily a spiritual gift and only secondarily a mental one. Its influence on the mental movements of its subject, although indirect, is not slight. It illuminates the mind as enthusiasm does, by stimulating and elevating it; it enriches the memory as

It is primarily a spiritual gift.

love does, by intensifying the interest in a certain object, and by making the mind sensitive
to its impressions and retentive of them. It
brings light to the understanding and wisdom
to the spirit, as purity of intention does, or as a
high aim in life does. Occasionally, as in the
case of Paul, it seizes upon a man of the largest
natural intellect and of rich attainment. But
so far as we can gather from the Bible, inspiration does not confer intellectual acuteness where
that did not previously exist, nor does it impart
superhuman power of knowing what ordinary
inquiry can ascertain. Luke, for example, was
not exempted from the necessity of making
inquiries, and, if in some points his informants
gave him information slightly differing from
the account we have in Mark, this only shows
us that inspiration was directed toward a different end from absolute uniformity in detail.
In the account given us of the creation, inspiration enabled the writer, not to give a description in which thousands of years afterward
perfect scientific accuracy might be found, but
to discover God in the work. And throughout
the Old Testament history it is not the *material*
which inspiration guarantees, but the spirit.
Many of the histories there recorded might
have done endless harm had they been recorded

in another spirit, in the spirit that glories in vice, revels in sensuality, and finds the devil everywhere. Recorded as they are, by inspired men, God is seen everywhere, vice is made dangerous and abhorrent, and the training of mankind by the Heavenly Father elucidated. This is primarily what inspiration gives. The Spirit of God in the man observing perceives and responds to the same Spirit in God revealing. Inspiration enables its possessor to see and apprehend God and His will, and to impart to other men what he has himself seen and apprehended; but of any further power it confers it is precarious to make assertions.

3. Within this one great function of inspiration considerable variety exists. The inspiration of Isaiah or Paul is different from that of the compiler of Proverbs or the annalist who drew up Chronicles. The work intrusted to one inspired man may be very different from that intrusted to another, and we are not to suppose that because their work is equally inspired it is equally profitable. Look at the Bible of an unsophisticated Christian and you at once see proof that some parts are more profitable than others. The Psalms, the Gospel of John, the Epistles, are blackened and illegible with use, while the book of Leviticus or Prov-

Variety in inspired products.

erbs is clean and crisp. In the human body there are essential or vital organs without which human life cannot be maintained, and there are parts which are of less importance. So in Scripture there are parts essential to its being and to its fulfilment of its purpose, and parts essential to its completeness.

Purpose of inspiration.

4. But this brings us to consider the *purpose* for which inspiration is given. It is not a superfluous gift which has served no purpose or a purpose which could have been served by man's unaided faculty. If Scripture is inspired, this is because there was a necessity for inspiration; and the inspiration of Scripture will be of a kind to correspond to this necessity. Now the necessity which called for inspiration was the necessity of having the self-manifestations of God understood and brought into contact with human knowledge and human wants. This being the purpose of inspiration, we may conclude that it fulfils this purpose, and that we have in Scripture a trustworthy record of the revelation of God and His will. And when the word "plenary" is used of inspiration to convey the idea that the inspiration of the writers of Scripture was sufficient to enable them to fulfil this purpose, then plainly the affirmation of the plenary inspiration of Scrip-

ture is legitimate. But if by "plenary inspiration" it be meant that every phrase and letter of Scripture is of Divine authority, this definition cannot be sustained by what we know of the purpose for which inspiration was given. For that inspiration being given to enable men to record the revelation of God and His will, if this is accomplished, the purpose and function of inspiration are accomplished; and we have no reason to suppose that inspiration will impart to its possessors keener insight into matters which cannot be included in the category of such as pertain to the revelation of God and His will.

V

INFALLIBILITY

V

INFALLIBILITY

It would be idle here to attempt a sketch of the work which criticism has accomplished in connection with the Gospels. The investigations of Abbott and Sanday and Carpenter, of Wright and Wilkinson, Woods and Zahn and Schmiedel, and especially of Sir John Hawkins and Wernle, are widely known and their results easily accessible. It may be presumed that every one who is in any degree interested in the subject is aware of the findings arrived at and of the history by which they have been reached. It may be presumed that we are all more or less convinced that the earliest evangelic documents now traceable are the reminiscences of Peter recorded by Mark, perhaps in a form slightly different from that of the second Gospel; and a book of Logia, which may approximately be recovered and which at any rate is embodied in Matthew and Luke. It must also be taken for granted that our own perusal of the Gospels has justified to our minds the pronouncements of criticism regarding the general relations of the Gospels and their individual characteristics; that Mark has been used both by the first and the third evangelist, and that while Matthew (or the first evangelist) writes for Jews to convince them of our Lord's Messiahship, and manifests a tendency to group both events and discourses, Luke shows a disposition to embellish the simplicity of his predecessor, and, writing for a man of education with a Gentile upbringing, selects his material accordingly.

By-products of criticism. But in pursuance of its object to discover the origin, character, and relations of the Gospels, criticism has thrown off some by-products, and it is with these we now have to do. The most important of these we must, however, meanwhile neglect. Nothing influences more profoundly the criticism of the Gospels than the presupposition of the incredibility of miracles. This alters entirely the character of the life of our Lord and necessitates the branding of the evangelists as incompetent. No literary or purely historical criticism cuts so deep into the Gospels as this. But any defence of the miraculous involves more than it is possible here to discuss; and, besides, it appears to me that it will be of greater service to attend to matters connected with Gospel criticism which are actually disturbing the faith of some of the members of the Church who have never doubted that our Lord's life was in some respects miraculous.

Among the results of the more careful examination of Scripture some have been subversive of previously conceived ideas of its infallibility. Criticism with a virtually unanimous voice declares that literal inerrancy cannot be claimed for the books either of the Old or New Testament. That the *substance* of the history is correct has been proved in a very remarkable manner by the unearthing and deciphering of long-buried records, written by non-Palestinian races yet confirming the Hebrew annals in their main particulars. But the same criticism which has made good use of those ancient records and monuments to confirm the statements of the Bible has also pointed out certain errors in chronology and in some other details. Restricting ourselves to the New Testament and to the Gospels, and to the universally admitted results of criticism, it has been put beyond all reasonable doubt that there exist irreconcilable discrepancies between the four accounts of some of our Lord's sayings and actions, and that it is impossible to determine, save on grounds of

Criticism repudiates literal inerrancy

probability, which Gospel we should follow. One or two examples selected at random will suffice. No two evangelists agree in their report of the title on the cross, or in their account of the appearances of our Lord after the resurrection. According to Mark and Luke, the women brought spices to anoint the body, when it had already been in the sepulchre for two nights and a day; according to John, Joseph of Arimathæa and Nicodemus had already anointed the body before placing it in the sepulchre. According to Mark, Luke, and John the women found the stone already rolled away from the entrance to the tomb; according to Matthew this was accomplished by an angel in presence of the women. The narrative of the events accompanying the resurrection, as it exists in Matthew, is generally irreconcilable with that of the other Gospels. Even in regard to the date of the last supper and the crucifixion the Gospels differ. Sometimes very puzzling discrepancies occur in the report of sayings which have a direct bearing upon the conduct of life. For example, in Matt. xix. 9, we read, " Whosoever shall put away his wife, except for fornication, and shall marry another, committeth adultery." But in Luke this great law is given without any exception, " Whosoever putteth away his wife, and marrieth another, committeth adultery." Which of these two very diverse laws ought the Church to follow? Not only are the Gospels at variance with one another in certain passages, but the individual writers seem not to have been exempt from liability to error. Mark quotes Malachi under the name of Isaiah; and Matthew ascribes to Jeremiah words spoken by Zechariah.

Now there are three methods of dealing with these and other more serious findings of criticism. The first is to deny the existence of these or any errors. The second is to admit the errors and to infer from their existence that the Bible is untrustworthy, not infallible. The third is to admit the errors while at the same time maintaining and exhibiting the infallibility of the Bible notwithstanding. *Three methods of treating discrepancies.*

The first method seems likely to blind men to the true nature of the Bible and to lead to disingenuousness, mischief, and unbelief. The second method is the result of ignorance, and especially of a misunderstanding of infallibility. The third gives us a sure standing ground and leads us to recognize the actual infallibility of Scripture. It can, I think, be demonstrated that although we grant to criticism all it *First method.*

claims, the Bible remains the infallible and
authoritative word of God; that, in fact, it
is independent of criticism.   As Professor
Stevens of Yale long ago said, "Amid all
the controversies about the Bible and the at-
tacks upon it, the Christian heart may rest
secure in this conviction, that the unique character and value of the Bible are as secure as
are the unique character and significance of the
person of Christ." [1]   It is a common presumption nowadays that the Bible has been discredited by criticism ; that like some old and
musty document preserved for ages in a sacred
obscurity, it has crumbled to dust as soon as
frankly exposed to the light of day; that it
has been so riddled with the shot and shell of
modern scientific warfare as to be on the point
of sinking.   But this involves a misunderstanding of the Bible and of the secret of its infallibility.   Modern assaults have developed new
methods of defence and a fresh perception of
the real strength of the Bible.   Until criticism
made it impossible for us any longer to identify

[1] " Doctrine and Life," p. 58.   Cf. Professor Wood's
"A Tenable Theory of Inspiration " : " The Bible can never
be replaced until some history has been produced that shall
reveal God more clearly than the history of Israel and of
the first Christian century.   A better book than the Bible
cannot be written until a better life than that of Christ has
been lived."

infallibility with literal inerrancy, it was a delusive and non-existent infallibility that was ascribed to the Bible. But now the real seat and character of its infallibility is discovered, and it is found to be an infallibility that can never be taken away from it.

How this is so we shall shortly see. But first, a word or two on the spurious infallibility or literal inerrancy of Scripture.

I have said that with a practically unanimous voice criticism declares that Scripture is not absolutely free from error. It may be said that no *critic* of repute denies that, in more or fewer particulars, mistake of more or less magnitude has crept in. There are, however, *theologians* of repute who maintain that every statement of the Bible is infallibly accurate ; that whether it be science or chronology or history that is touched upon, all is absolutely inerrant. Drs. Hodge and Warfield, for example, men of wide learning and well-earned theological repute, maintain that God presided over the sacred writers in their entire work of writing, " with the design and effect of making that writing an errorless record." [1] And again, " A proved error in Scripture contradicts not only our doctrine, but the Bible claims, and therefore its

Criticism declares against inerrancy of Scripture.

[1] *Presbyterian Review*, Vol. II.

inspiration in making these claims." [1] And not
a few less distinguished persons declare that
their salvation depends on the absolute accuracy of every word from the first in Genesis to
the last in Revelation. Happily their salvation
depends on nothing of the kind, but on a living
Person whom we can know and trust if the
Gospels are no more trustworthy than Plutarch
or Tacitus, or any ordinary history or biography. If Matthew affirms that Jesus was
asked by the people, Is it lawful to heal on
the Sabbath-day ? while in point of fact, as
another Gospel tells us, it was He who put that
question to them, is my salvation thereby im-
perilled ? If we are told in Samuel that the
price paid for Araunah's threshing floor was
fifty silver shekels, while in Chronicles we are
told that it was six hundred gold shekels, does
this prevent my perceiving that Christ reveals
God and accepting that revelation? To me the
assertion seems simply monstrous. And that
intelligent Christian men should avow that
their faith hangs on so precarious a tenure is a
most significant circumstance.

*Recoil from
claim of
inerrancy.*

This uneasiness about the inerrancy of Scripture in all matters of detail is worthy of attention, because many are seriously disturbed by

[1] *Presbyterian Review*, Vol. II., p. 245.

the results of criticism and in some instances
the recoil from a belief in the infallible accuracy of Scripture has had disastrous consequences. It is truly said that "the man who
binds up the cause of Christianity with the
literal accuracy of the Bible is no friend of
Christianity, for with the rejection of that
theory too often comes the rejection of the
Bible itself, and faith is shattered."[1] In Renan's case this was the result. He tells us in
his "Recollections"[2] that he had been brought
up in the belief that it was essential to the orthodox doctrine of Scripture to accept it as inerrant in every line. When he entered upon the
study of the history of Israel he soon discovered that such a claim was untenable, and accordingly parted company with the Church.
So, too, Charles Bradlaugh, from an ingenuous

[1] Snell, "Gain or Loss," p. 20.

[2] "In a divine book everything must be true, and as two
contradictions cannot both be true, it must not contain
any contradiction. But the careful study of the Bible which
I had undertaken, while revealing to me many historical and
æsthetic treasures, proved to me also that it was not more
exempt than any other ancient book from contradictions,
inadvertencies, and errors." — RENAN, "Recollections,"
p. 256.

"The mildest Catholic doctrine as to inspiration will not
allow one to admit there is any marked error in the sacred
text, or any contradiction in matters which do not relate
either to faith or morality " (p. 257).

and inquiring youth, was turned into a bitter opponent of the faith because a kind of faith in Scripture was demanded of him which he could not honestly give. The whole force of Ingersoll's arguments, by means of which he turned hundreds from Christianity, depends on an acceptance of the literal and total infallibility of Scripture. Given a true view of Scripture, his whole contention falls to the ground. Those who maintain that we must accept every statement of Scripture, or none of it, should consider that no doctrine more surely manufactures sceptics. " It seems," says Dr. Stearns, "a very good and pious thing to insist that the Bible is absolutely without error. But nothing is good or pious that is contrary to facts." And to those who avow that their faith hangs upon the infallibility of the letter, nothing better can be said than what was indignantly said by Frederick Denison Maurice : " I will not believe any Christian man, even upon his own testimony, who tells me that he should cease to trust in the Son of God, because he found chronological or historical misstatements in the Scriptures, as great as ever have been charged against them by their bitterest opponents. If I did suspect him of such hollowness, I should pray for him that he might never meet with any travellers or

philologers who confirmed the statements of
Scripture, none but such as denied them or
mocked at them, because the sooner such a
foundation is shaken, the better it will be for
them."

I have said that the denial of errors in the
Gospels leads men to a disingenuous treatment
of the narratives. If they find that one Gospel
relates the healing of one blind man as Jesus
entered Jericho, while another relates the cure
of two blind men on His leaving it, the harmo-
nizer at once steps forward and solves the dis-
crepancy by affirming that of course three blind
men were healed, — the one at the entrance,
the others at the exit. This he will do notwithstanding the fact that it is Matthew's habit
to duplicate, and regardless of the similarity or
we may say identity of the narratives in other
respects, — in the pause made by Jesus on the
road, in the question He puts, and in the answer
He receives. This I think may, without harsh-
ness, be called disingenuous, and moreover it
turns attention away from the feature of the
narratives which prompted its recital, the fact,
not that Jesus was at the one gate or the other
of the city, for that is of no significance, but
that He was addressed as Son of David. That
in some instances the Gospels complete one

*Disingenu-
ous treat-
ment of
Gospels.*

another is no doubt true; but this harmonizing by simple addition is a method which may very easily betray us, and which at any rate becomes quite useless when the Gospels contradict one another.

No literally infallible Scripture.   Another method of evading the acknowledgment of error, if not disingenuous, is thoughtless. I refer to the method of shifting the claim of infallibility from Scripture as we have it, to Scripture as it came from the writer's hand. This is a vain subterfuge, and it is based upon a misunderstanding of the character of the errors alleged. These errors are not such as could be introduced into the text by the blunders of copyists. They are not confined to single words or lines. Such errors in numbers or names may exist in the Old Testament. But in the Gospels the misstatements pointed out by criticism are such as could only have been made by the original writers. The subterfuge is based, then, upon a misapprehension. But also it is idle. For what possible use to us can an infallible Scripture be which has long since passed out of existence? If a Scripture literally infallible is necessary to salvation, where is it to be found? We know that our present texts are only an approximation to what was originally written. We cannot be quite sure in every case that this or that was the word used by an apostle or spoken by our Lord. This demand, in short, for a literally infallible Scripture cannot by any possibility be satisfied.

The reluctance to admit the existence of errors in Scripture is not surprising, and is even in a sense commendable. It arises from our natural instinct to reverence and exalt those who have been the organs of revelation, and in a manner mediators between God and us. Knowing how much we owe them, we cannot bear to ascribe to them any least degree of faultiness. When Peter and Paul disagree, we turn away from the quarrel, and refuse to draw the necessary inference that Peter did his best to mislead the Church on a matter of vital importance. *Natural reluctance to admit error.*

More powerful even than this wholesome Christian instinct the misunderstanding of *inspiration* and its results has led Christian people to believe in the infallibility of the writers of Scripture. Inspiration is the indwelling of the Divine Spirit. All Christians believe that they themselves enjoy this indwelling, but they are not conscious of becoming infallible. Some of the men who have most fully possessed the Spirit of Christ have been profoundly ignorant *Results of inspiration.*

persons.   *A priori* we cannot affirm *what* results inspiration will have in the writers of
Scripture.   How far it produced a more accurate knowledge of things external and non-
essential we can only gather from examination
of the actual results as found in their writings.
Certainly a high degree of inspiration, such as
that enjoyed by Paul, brings a man into a close
fellowship with Christ; and his experience of
the source, the graciousness, the power, and the
joy of that fellowship gives him knowledge of
the true eternal relation of the soul to Christ
fitted to make him an authoritative teacher of
others.   But the full indwelling of the Holy
Spirit, the " inspiration " of Paul or of Stephen,
did not prevent them from stumbling in dates
and details.

*Inspiration
one thing,
infallibility
another.*

Looking, then, at the facts of Scripture, we
see that inspiration is one thing, infallibility
another.   Presumably the writers of the books
of Kings and Chronicles were inspired, yet it
is matter of common knowledge that many
discrepancies exist in these books.   Professor
Sayce, one of the most conservative of living
critics, tells us that " Assyrian inscriptions have
shown that the chronology of the book of
Kings is hopelessly wrong."   We also find
that the historical writers of the Old Testa-

ment refer to older documents as their authorities, precisely as secular historians depend on national archives and contemporary accounts. And if inspiration did not give a direct knowledge of past events, but left inspired writers to depend on contemporary witnesses, is it credible that inspiration would enable them to detect mistakes in those older writers? If inspiration gave the latter species of insight, one does not see why it should not have given the former.

Throughout the New Testament also there is evidence that inspiration did not render its subjects infallible in their criticism or lift them above the level of contemporary knowledge. Jude, an inspired man, cites the apocryphal book of Enoch, written shortly before his own time, as if it were the utterance of the antediluvian who walked with God. All the writers expected the speedy return of Christ— an expectation which events have proved to be erroneous. In short, the facts of Scripture put it beyond doubt that inspiration does not involve infallibility.

Admitting, then, the finding of criticism that inerrancy cannot be claimed for the Gospels or for Scripture generally, we go on to ask how this affects the infallibility of Scripture. It *Inaccuracies of Scripture are slight.*

is this which lends interest to the subject.
For, apart from the error ascribed to the Gospels on account of their narration of supposed
miracles, the misstatements found in them are
trifling. None of them are such as to make
the reader feel uncertain about the trustworthiness or general accuracy of the writers. Indeed, no one can fail to be struck with the
manner in which they stand the tests which fresh
discoveries are from year to year applying to
their accuracy. For example, the topographical
errors so freely ascribed to the fourth Gospel
a few years ago are now, since the Palestinian
Survey, no more heard of. The inaccuracies
which do occur are so trifling that one feels
ashamed to point them out. They are the
little cracks or miniature crevasses in the continuous surface of the glacier which are unnoticed and taken in the stride of the honest
wayfarer bent on attaining the summit. If the
pedestrian wantonly thrusts his foot into a
hole, he may twist his ankle and prevent
further progress, but for the honest man they
present no real break, hindrance, or pitfall.

Why notice them?

Why, then, notice them? We are compelled
to notice them, partly because without recognizing the facts of the Bible we cannot hope to
reach any just conception of its nature ; partly

because it is necessary to call attention to the insignificance of these discrepancies; but mainly because they lead us to distinguish between a spurious infallibility and that which is genuine.

Before going on to exhibit the genuine infallibility of Scripture, it may be well to ask what grounds we have for demanding or expecting an infallible guide in religion, of the kind that is sought in the Bible. The craving for such a guide arises from two sources. The first is the shrinking from responsibility which characterizes not all men, but the vast majority. Various are the devices by which men have sought to evade the burden of self-determination: the lot, the oracle, supposed providences, the merest turn of a coin or opening of a book, anything which will give them a pretext for trusting some other impulse than that of their own reason. *The craving for infallible guide.*

The second source of this craving is the supposed need of a judge in controversies. So long as a man uses the Bible only to find his own way to God, it does not occur to him that any stringent theory of infallibility is required. He seeks for God, and he finds Him. It is only when he begins to urge his views upon others, and becomes impatient at the slowness with which conviction grows in them, that he seeks *For a judge in controversies.*

an irresistible authority that compels submission. It is, at bottom, unbelief in spiritual forces. An external, irresistible authority is sought, — an authority easily accessible and easily applied, — as if men could not be trusted to recognize truth when they see it, or even to wish to find God.

Common liability to error.

In other departments of knowledge men have been allowed to sift the false from the true at the greatest expenditure of time and of life ; they have been allowed to make mistakes and to follow those mistakes to their issues; they have been allowed to sacrifice thousands of human lives in every generation to mistaken ideas. It may be urged that in religion the consequence of error is so grave that it cannot be supposed men should be left to any uncertainty here. But in point of fact the majority of men have been left in ignorance, or with only such witness to God's existence and goodness as could be available for those who were prepared to search, to sift, to think, to act.

No evasion of responsibility possible.

Escape from all possibility of error and from the responsibility of determining our own future is impossible whether we choose the Church as our infallible guide, or Scripture, or Christ Himself; it must be *our* choice that is exercised, our judgment that determines this great step. We cannot get behind ourselves and find some other spring of action than our own determination. It must be by the response of our own conscience to Christ's personality and words that we choose Him as our ultimate authority. The testimony of others may aid us: the Gospels are necessary to show us what He is and to preserve to us His true image and His very claims; but it is we ourselves who must for ourselves determine whether this Person is what He claims to be.

But the main question for us is, What is the infallibility which may be claimed for Scripture and especially for the Gospels? Many persons lightly claim infallibility for Scripture without once asking themselves the question, "Infallible for what?" The whole matter hinges here. What is the infallibility we claim for the Bible? Is it infallibility in grammar, in style, in history, in science, or what? *Its infallibility must be determined by its purpose.* If you say that your watch is infallible, you mean, as a time-keeper; — not that it has a flawless case, not that it will tell you the day of the month, or predict to-morrow's weather. The navigator finds his chart infallible as a guide to lighthouses, and shallows, and sunken rocks, but useless to give him the time of day or to inform him of the

Nature of infallibility determined by purpose of Scripture.

products and prices of the land he is bound for. A guide may infallibly lead you over a difficult and not easily found pass, although he is ignorant of any language but his own and knows little that happens beyond his own mountains.

Purpose of Scripture.

What, then, is the purpose of the Bible? Its purpose is to exhibit Christ. As our Lord Himself defined the Scriptures, "They are they which testify of me." By means of the Scriptures the knowledge of God's saving love in Christ is communicated to the world. It was not God's purpose to teach science or ethnology by them, nor to give us knowledge of matters about which men are always curious, such as the conditions of a future life; it was not His purpose to make us theological experts, — else He had signally failed, — but His purpose was to set Christ before men in living grace and majesty, and so perpetuate the knowledge of Him upon earth. In Christ we have the supreme revelation of God, and if Scripture conveys to us a sufficient knowledge of Christ, it accomplishes its purpose. Luther was right when he said, "That is not Scripture which does not exhibit Christ."

Minor errors no difficulty.

Now no sooner do we grasp this conception of Scripture than we recognize that discrepancies in the Gospels, or errors in other parts of

the Bible, are of no consequence at all as affecting the account given us of Christ. The four
Gospels differ from one another in this or that
part of their narrative, but it is the same Christ
which each exhibits. The trustworthiness of
the Gospels is guaranteed both by the agreement, in the main, of these four accounts, and
by the fact that the ordinary Christian has
never found any difficulty in forming one consistent image of Christ out of the four accounts.
The discrepancies only become dangerous when
they are used as a lever to subvert the infallibility of Scripture. And they are frequently
thus used by persons who take advantage of
the claim of literal infallibility advanced by
well-intentioned but inconsiderate persons. This
claim of literal infallibility is easily disposed of
by means of these discrepancies — here are clear
instances in which it is impossible to claim this
kind of infallibility ; and hence the inference
is at once drawn that the Bible is not in any
sense infallible. The inference is utterly un-
justifiable. Literal infallibility is not that for
which we contend ; and these discrepancies
might be multiplied a hundred fold and yet
avail nothing to discredit the true infallibility
of Scripture. And this for two reasons : —

1. Unimportant errors in detail are never suf-

fered to discredit a historian. The rule "falsus in uno, falsus in omnibus" is valid in the law courts as applicable to a witness who is found intentionally distorting truth. A witness on oath who, with intent to deceive, withholds or perverts truth is of course discredited in the whole of his testimony. But the maxim has no application to ordinary life or to the writing of history. For there is no man who has not occasionally stumbled into error, — error at once condoned and which reflects no shadow on his general reputation for truth. Tacitus has been found in error, but we do not on that account read his Annals or his Histories with a watchful suspicion. There is no historian who has not been proved in error; but occasional, unintentional, and unimportant error is lost to view in the general reputation for accuracy which the historian acquires.

2. And, secondly, if it be said, is not all error important where Divine truth and eternal interests are concerned? we answer, No! else God would have provided for the absence of all error. Error is unimportant when it does not affect the purpose of the whole. Errors in grammar are of no consequence when the meaning remains intelligible and the sense unaffected. No errors in Scripture are of importance which

do not prevent it from accomplishing God's purpose of preserving for us the knowledge of His revelation in Christ. It must be judged by its fulfilment of its object, and its object was to enable us to apprehend God in Christ and lead us to Him. This object it has infallibly accomplished. Men who have devoutly sought God in Christ have found him. The Christian ages stand behind us with their irrefutable testimony. The Scriptures have infallibly led men to Christ. They have fulfilled the function which Christ ascribed to them. They have set before men a Christ in whom God is found.

It is perhaps worth while to adduce the testimony of one or two authorities on this subject. *Testimonies to Scripture.* The last century produced no more daring and untrammelled thinker than Heine, no man less controlled or influenced by other men's faiths and opinions, but we find him saying, " He that has lost his God can find Him again in this book, and toward him who has never known Him it wafts the breath of the Divine word." After Dr. Martineau has cut away from the Gospels ten times more than a sober criticism warrants, he is still constrained to say, " No one can affect ignorance of what Jesus was; enough is saved to plant His personality in a clear space, distinct from all that history, or even fiction,

presents."[1] Still more definitely Robertson
Smith: "So long as we go to Scripture only to
find in it God and His redeeming love mirrored
before the eye of faith, we may rest assured
that we shall find living, self-evidencing, infallible truth in every part of it, and that we shall
find nothing else. . . . Since Scripture has no
other end than to convey to us a message which,
when accompanied by the inner witness of the
Spirit, manifests itself as the infallible word of
God, we may for practical purposes say that
Scripture is the infallible word of God."

*Touchstone
of Scrip-
ture.*

Here we reach the true touchstone of Scripture. Why do I receive it as the word of
God? Is it because the Church certifies it and
assures me it is infallible? But the Church
herself is not infallible, and she may be in error
in this as she has been elsewhere. Is it because
Scripture itself claims infallibility? But Scripture does not; and if it did, how do I know I
should believe it? Many have claimed to be
Divine messengers who have been proved false.
*The only possible ultimate ground for believing
Scripture to be the word of God is that there is
that in the truth delivered which convinces me
that God is its Author.* In the last resort you
must depend solely on your own conviction

[1] "Seat of Authority," p. 607.

that here God speaks to you. If there is not a self-evidencing power in Christ and in His revelation, you will never find evidence of His truth anywhere else.

It would seem that the members of our churches are yet far from understanding that the authentication of Christ cannot be touched by criticism; that He is His own best witness, and that this witness is independent of any doctrine or theory of the inspiration or infallibility of Scripture. That Christ has given to the world the highest idea of God ever promulgated, that the conscience of every man who is brought into His presence acknowledges Christ as the best and divinest he knows or can conceive — these are incontestable facts. Before we form any opinion about the Gospels, and even though we see much in them that we cannot accept, they set before us this unique figure — a figure far beyond the creative power of the writers and carrying in it its own authentication, its own direct appeal to heart and conscience and reason. We need as little fear the nibblings of criticism as we fear the minute erosions of our shores by the ocean. The knowledge of God actually conveyed to all who read the Gospels cannot be taken away, and that knowledge is life eternal.

Christ is self-authenticating.

The two extreme positions, then, are alike untenable. It is impossible to maintain the infallibility of Scripture on the ground of its literal accuracy in every one of its statements; and it is impossible to deny the infallibility of Scripture as a spiritual guide on the ground that there are found in it certain errors and discrepancies. Our acceptance of Scripture as the word of God depends, not on its absolute freedom from error of every kind, but on our recognition of God's voice in it. Criticism may work its will on the books of the New Testament; it cannot take from us the Christ they embody. That figure is self-certifying as it was to those who knew Him while He dwelt on earth. As a great German critic whose work was prematurely cut short has said: "The man who refers Christianity to Scripture as the fundamental witness of Christ, assumes on that very account an attitude of inner freedom toward its historical form, because he has found Christ in it, and because he judges all that is in it from this central point. If we are sure of this, that Scripture in its entire contents witnesses of Christ, then we are no longer puzzled about the worth of Scripture, even though here or there we meet with irregularities over which we cannot make our way. If we are sure that

God's Spirit speaks to us in Scripture, then we
are no longer timidly anxious when historical
investigations into the persons of the human
composers are set on foot. The determining
fact abides, that the living God, the God of our
salvation, in Scripture speaks to us of Christ,
whoever be the human author who here or
there with heart and hand has put himself at
His service." [1]

It only remains that a brief answer be given
to the questions put by the somewhat puzzled
average man. To transfer one's faith from a
literally infallible Scripture to an infallible
Christ is not an absolutely easy undertaking,
and difficulties arise in the process. It has,
for example, been asked, " Can a fallible Scripture infallibly lead to Christ?" "If we have
no infallible record, we have no guarantee of
an infallible Christ." Enough has already
been said to explain how a Scripture, which is
not in one sense and for one purpose infallible,
may be infallible in another sense and for
another purpose. Enough has been said to
show that Gospels of which we cannot affirm
absolute inerrancy do yet set before us a self-
verifying Christ. The pilot who has never
lost a ship, and who is practically infallible

*Difficulties
of the aver-
age man.*

[1] Gloel, " Die jungste Kritik," p. 96.

within his own domain, may yet believe in mermaids and sea serpents, may never have heard of Cromwell or Milton or Washington, and may think brandy a cure for every human ill.

Scripture always judged by the Christian reader.

Again, it is frequently said, If there is the slightest error in Scripture, then I must judge for myself what I am to receive, and how am I to find out what is true and what is misleading? It may, I think, fairly be replied, This is precisely what every one who reads the Bible is already doing. And the fact that men are not aware that they thus judge Scripture for themselves proves how little serious consideration they have given to the subject. Who is at the reader's elbow as he peruses Exodus and Leviticus to tell him what is of permanent authority and what was for the Mosaic economy only? Who whispers to us as we read Genesis and Kings, This is exemplary; this is not? Who sifts for us the speeches of Job and enables us to treasure as Divine truth what he utters in one verse, while we reject the next as Satanic raving? Who gives the preacher authority and accuracy of aim to pounce on a sound text in Ecclesiastes, while wisdom and folly toss and roll over one another in confusingly rapid and inextricable contortions? What enables the humblest Christian to come safely through the cursing Psalms and go straight to forgive his enemy? What tells us we may eat things strangled, though the whole college of apostles deliberately and expressly prohibited such eating? Who assures us we need not anoint the sick with oil, although in the New Testament we are explicitly commanded to do so? In a word, how is it that the simplest reader can be trusted with the Bible and can be left to find his own spiritual nourishment in it, rejecting almost as much as he receives? Paul solves the whole matter for us in his bold and exhaustive words, " The spiritual man — the man who has the spirit of Christ — judgeth all things." This, and this only, is the true touchstone of Scripture by which all things are tried. To use the words of one of the most thoughtful writers of our time, " It is the same spirit which has embodied truth in the Bible that infuses the love of truth into the Christian; and no magnetism gives more assurance of its reality in material things than such sympathy gives in spiritual, that the sincere seeker shall ultimately find all such truth in the Bible as there is a moral fitness, or necessity, that he should possess." [1]

[1] Myers, "Catholic Thoughts," p. 132.

*How is the
plain man
to judge?*

If, then, it still be asked, How is the plain man to distinguish? How is the man in the street to know what is true? How can you refer him to the word of God if there are statements in it which may misinform him? the reply is, No statement will mislead the man who is honestly seeking his way to God. If it is spiritual guidance the man is in search of, then you may refer him absolutely to the Bible. To scruple to do so, because the Gospels disagree in their accounts of Christ's resurrection, or because, possibly, 2 Peter is a forgery, is grotesquely absurd. If a man desires to acquaint himself with the history of the ancient world, there are other books to which you would more naturally refer him; but if he seeks enlightenment regarding the preparation made by history for the coming of Christ, you would refer him to the Bible. If he seeks information regarding the formation of this globe, and the introduction of life upon it, there are works in palæontology which will satisfy him; but if he desires to be impressed with the relation of God to the world and its life, you will refer him to Genesis. If he craves a knowledge of the times of Christ, there are other books he may profitably consult; but if he wishes to know Christ, and through this ultimate revelation to see the Father, you do not hesitate to say, In the Gospels you will find what you seek. It is idle to assert that if we cannot say of each clause of the Bible, "This is infallibly true," we cannot refer to the Bible as the Word of God at all. With the most perfect freedom we can refer to it every man who is seeking infallible guidance to God. "Try to treat the volumes as a flawless chronological or scientific record, and you will be disappointed. Treat it as a means of religious edification, and you cannot fail." [1]

[1] Snell, "Gain or Loss," p. 27.

VI

THE TRUSTWORTHINESS OF THE GOSPELS

VI

THE TRUSTWORTHINESS OF THE GOSPELS

THE present and pressing need of reconsider- *The critical method.*
ing the trustworthiness of the Gospels is too
obvious to call for much comment.   The need
arises from the emergence of a new *method* of
inquiry and new *material* for prosecuting it.

The new method is known as historical
criticism, — sometimes since Eichhorn's time
unhappily called "higher criticism,"—a method
which is really not in itself new, but is now
employed with much greater vigor and exact-
ness than in the past.   It is important to
observe that this method is *inevitable*.   The
popular suspicion or jealousy of it arises from
a misunderstanding of its nature, its aims, its
instruments.   Sometimes it is even spoken of
as antagonistic to Christianity.   It is identified
with certain of its manifestations, and is forth-
with condemned.   But the abuse of an instrument or method does not nullify or condemn
its legitimate use.   The erroneous conclusions

of scientific inquiry can only be corrected by
further and more searching inquiry of the same
scientific character. Criticism is not a hostile
force hovering round the march of the Christian Church, picking off all loosely attached
followers and galling the main body; it is
rather the highly trained corps of scouts and
skirmishers thrown out on all sides to ascertain
in what direction it is safe and possible for
the Church to advance. Our attitude toward
criticism should not be that of grudging and
reluctant submission as to an unfortunate epi-
demic; rather we should welcome it as we
welcome convalescence. It is the convenient
designation of the most approved methods of
ascertaining historical truth. It is a process
of which every inquirer, more or less con-
sciously, avails himself. Every living man
has his own tests which he applies to all he
hears or reads; and by these tests he determines
whether or not belief is warranted. If a sailor
tells us he found oranges growing among the
ice-hummocks of the Arctic circle we refuse
to believe him, because his information is
tested and condemned by the knowledge we
already possess. If a document professing to
belong to the age of Queen Anne makes free
reference to electric lighting, telephones, or

photography, we know that its claim is spurious. In short, every man is necessarily a critic, and criticism as a science collects and applies all the criteria which experience has approved for the determination of the dates of documents, of their character and credibility, and for discriminating between what is to be accepted as historical and what must be regarded as fabricated or embellished. Without criticism it is impossible we should reach the very truth about the Gospels or any other ancient documents. By allowing criticism within our gates, we no doubt admit a treatment of the Gospels which some will take advantage of to get rid of everything which does not suit their conception of Christ and His teaching. But this is a state of matters we must face. We must examine objections and difficulties in detail with candor, patience, and a determination to reach the truth. How do those who decline the severest scrutiny propose to find what the Gospels actually are?

The novelty of the *material* furnished to the critic of our time is more striking than the novelty of the method. For the knowledge of the past the critic is now provided with an apparatus which has never before been within his reach. Archæology, history, anthropology, *Critical material* psychology,— each makes its distinct contribution toward the ascertainment of the real condition and events of long past periods in the life of man.

Archæological material.

Archæology brings its quota, exhuming the ancient world which so long has lain buried out of sight and knowledge, and bringing a revivified past before the mind.   Inscriptions, monuments, excavated cities, thousands of papyri from Egyptian tombs and ruined villages and crocodile cemeteries, the brick libraries of the valley of the Euphrates, put in the hands of scholars material for the reconstruction of the ancient world such as never before has been available.   We are thus furnished with a new means of testing the accuracy and ascertaining the true character of parts of the Old Testament.   The discovery of legends very similar to those which occupy the early chapters of Genesis cannot but be used for the truer understanding of these records.   The facts brought to notice by palæontology, and even the inscribed monuments of ancient races, compel us considerably to expand the chronology of Scripture; while the doctrine of evolution suggests modifications of our idea of creation and the date of man's appearance on earth.

In the study of the Gospels we have now to

take into account a good deal that is either newly discovered or that has hitherto been disregarded. Miracles have found a new foe in evolution, which demands that every event in history be referred to causes previously existing in the world. No interruption of the rigid chain of cause and effect is permissible: no irruption from the outside. This prohibition of the miraculous is buttressed by the examination of the biographies of saints and founders of religion; for this has brought to light that not to Jesus only have miracles been ascribed by enthusiastic followers, but to Buddha and to the Bab, and even to Thomas à Becket and St. Francis of Assisi, and many besides. The *comparative* study of miracles has been introduced and has necessitated a revised defence.

Comparative religion.

Again, anthropologists have taught us that at a certain stage of civilization all disease is referred to demoniacal possession, that at a somewhat higher stage certain diseases, such as epilepsy, neurasthenia, and mania, are so referred, and that in various countries, both in our own and other times, exorcism is practised. We cannot simply put these facts aside and aver that the demoniacal possession spoken of in the Gospels belongs to a different category.

Anthropology.

*Other sa-
cred books.*

The publication of the sacred books of other religions has had its effect, for in them we find stronger claims to inspiration and infallibility than we find in our own Scriptures. And it is quite fairly and pertinently asked: " How can such claims be disproved by arguments which are not equally applicable if urged by a Hindu against similar pretensions which may be raised on behalf of the Bible? "

*Necessary
inferences.*

Confronted, then, with these various facts, the candid student cannot but ask whether our Gospels belong to the class of somewhat untrustworthy and irresponsible biographies which have obscured the life of our greatest men ; whether they are just on the same plane as the records which embalm the memory of Buddha and the Bab, and must be subject to the same deductions if we are to reach the truth; or whether they carry in themselves notes of truth which command our confidence and incline us to believe, if not every event or word as recorded, yet the truthfulness of the portrait of Jesus they present.

*Criticism
cannot be
barred out.*

To turn this whole inquiry aside by the simple affirmation that the Gospels are inspired, and are therefore infallibly accurate in every detail, is in the highest degree mischievous. If infallibly accurate, then they need not shrink from the keenest criticism. But none of our Gospels professes to be infallible or even inspired. Only one of them tells us how its writer obtained his information, and that was by careful inquiry at the proper sources. But even though all of them claimed inspiration, this would not give us an answer to our question. The indwelling of the Spirit of God does not impart omniscience to the human mind, does not even impart knowledge of human history or science. It is only by examining the Gospels themselves that we can discover how far they are trustworthy. To attempt to bar out criticism by affirming inspiration is a futile enterprise. The day for that is past. You cannot now do it. Men will for themselves inquire and will test the accuracy of the Gospels because they are resolved to know the truth; for let us make no mistake, the freest inquiry is the only possible path to sound conviction. God's world is a world of progress; the tide is now flowing, and he who stiffly clings to his old moorings will inevitably be swamped. We must obey God's call and without fear let truth carry us where it leads.

The importance of having an *inspired* record consists in two of its results. (1) We have the ministry of Jesus recorded in the same *Results of inspiration.*

spirit in which it was enacted, by men sympathetic with His mind and intention.   We may
be sure that those features of His life are
recorded which He Himself considered significant.   We are not told the color of His hair or
the kind of clothes He wore; physical details
are absent, and the writers would be surprised
to learn how much the modern mind has made
of trifles.   But their inspiration assures us
that if Jesus was the Christ, this will be
brought out; and if He proclaimed deliverance
from sin, that will be recorded.   And (2) it
assures us that there is no *intentional* deception
in their narrative.   They present Christ as
they believed Him to be.   Error there may
be, but not deliberate misrepresentation.   The
writers, conscious of the greatness of their
theme, cannot but have desired to ascertain
the truth.   The very form of their narrative,
its freedom from all exclamatory or personal
matter, is proof that subjectivity was at its
minimum in them, that they were conscious of
a responsibility to the public and sought to
discharge it worthily.

We live in a
critical age.   No time, then, need be spent in exhibiting the
supreme *importance* of determining whether and
how far we can trust the Gospels ; still less in
deprecating or depreciating criticism, the only

instrument whose employment gives any promise of our reaching the truth. We might as well try to lift ourselves into the age of Homer as try to breathe an air not impregnated with criticism. The classics have been subjected to quite as severe an ordeal as the New Testament, and, as a great Greek scholar has said, "Against this onslaught, it is not surprising that the average scholar has taken refuge in deafness, or looked on with sympathetic hope, while Herbst does his magnificent gladiator-work in defence of everything he believed in the sixties — the time, as he plaintively says, when he felt, in opening his Thucydides, that he was 'resting in Abraham's bosom.'" For the intelligent student of the New Testament the "sixties" with their ingenuous methods are as irrevocably past as our own childhood, and from the unquestioning security of "Abraham's bosom," we have passed, for the time at least, into the cleansing fires of the critical purgatory.

But here again two cautions must be added. (1) Our hope is in criticism free, fair, full. But we have yet to search with a lantern for the ideal critic. Even the most circumspect of those who at present influence opinion cannot be acquitted of an occasional craving for novelty or of accepting possibilities as probabilities or

But the ideal critic has not yet appeared.

even as certainties. As the savage is not rated
as a man until he can produce a few scalps or
heads, so the Privat-Docent or budding theo-
logue hopes to win his spurs by fleshing his
sword on some well-established belief and is
not greatly concerned about the finality or
truth of his discoveries. This is accountable
for much ill-considered writing and an exasper-
ating waste of time for any one who tries to
keep pace with critical literature. But, what is
worse, it leads to partisanship and one-sidedness.

Criticism not peculiar to our time.
(2) A second caution seems continually disregarded. This age is characterized by criticism. A lack of originality turns the mind
keenly back upon the work done by former
ages. But too often critics speak as if their
methods were unknown to the ancient world
and that any statement was allowed to pass,
and no laws of evidence recognized. We hear
too much of " the trained historical critic," and
he is so flaunted as to reflect discredit on the
credulity of the ancient world. The result is
that we judge ancient writers with a preconceived idea that they were ready to accept and
give currency to idle tales. They are damaged
from the outset by this prejudice, and all that
is extraordinary in their narrative is set down
to their credulity.

But, while unquestionably criticism is culti-
vated now as it never has been before, it should
be borne in mind that the grounds of rational
belief are expressly laid down in the "Rhetoric"
of Aristotle and in the speeches of Demosthenes,
who directs the attention of the judges to the
distinction between circumstantial evidence, the
testimony of eye-witnesses, and mere probability. This was a necessary result of legal
procedure in such courts as those of Greece and
Rome. And how well the grounds of trustworthiness were understood by historians two
centuries before our Gospels were written is
illustrated in the preface of Polybius, who
states that he begins his history from the year
220 B.C., "because the period thus embraced
would fall partly in the life of my parents,
partly in my own ; and thus I should be able to
speak as eye-witness of some of the events and
of others from the information of eye-witnesses.
To go farther back and write the report of a
report, traditions at second or third hand
seemed to be unsatisfactory either with a view
to giving clear impressions or making sound
statements." And no one can read Polybius
without recognizing his bright intelligence, his
perception of the snares of the historian, his
critical discernment of the sources he may safely

*But culti-
vated in pre-
Christian
days.*

use. Take, for example, this description of
two of his predecessors : " I do not suppose
that these writers have intentionally stated what
was false ; but I think that they are much in
the same state of mind as men in love. Partisanship and complete prepossession made
Philinus think that all the actions of the Car-
thaginians were characterized by wisdom, courage, and honor, those of the Romans by the
reverse.. Fabius thought the exact opposite.
Now in other relations of life one would hesitate to exclude such warmth of sentiment ; for
a good man ought to be loyal to his friends and
patriotic to his country; ought to be at one with
his friends in their hatreds and likings. But
directly a man assumes the moral attitude of an
historian, he must forget all such considerations.
For, as a living creature is rendered quite useless if deprived of its eyes, so if you take truth
from history, what is left is but an idle, unprof-
itable tale." It may be added that the latest
editor of Polybius makes the following significant remark — which is not without application
to our subject : " That Polybius thoroughly
knew and carefully recorded the facts about
which he wrote might seem a truism hardly
worth stating, if it were not that it is so
wantonly forgotten whenever his authority

comes into collision with the last invented theory." [1]

The critic must, therefore, be on his guard against unduly widening the interval between modern and ancient methods and against the presumption that the writers of our Gospels questioned not at all, but set down all they heard. No doubt it remains to ask how far this regard to sufficient evidence, which is found in some ancient writers, penetrated the minds of those who compiled our Gospels. But certainly the authors of the third and fourth Gospels appreciated the value of eye-witness; and by their explicit manifestation of this appreciation they reveal not merely their individual estimate of its value but the sense of it cherished by the community. In a word, if we would reach the truth, we must not start with the wholly unwarranted assumption that the Gospel writers were credulous and incompetent, ready to accept all they heard and to set down as fact whatever they fancied would magnify their hero. *Were the evangelists credulous?*

In proceeding, then, to inquire into the trustworthiness of the Gospels, it must first of all be clearly apprehended that by trustworthiness we do not mean perfect accuracy in every *Object of the Gospels.*

[1] Strachan-Davidson, "Polybius," p. x.

detail, but a faithful fulfilment of their purpose to perpetuate the true image of Christ.
It has been over and over again demonstrated
that minute accuracy cannot be claimed for the
Gospels.   What we contend for is that *these
documents preserve a true picture of Him whose
ministry they describe.*   A nibbling criticism has
done much, and may do more, to eat away some
elements in the Gospel story, but the question
is, Can it so eat it away as to leave us without
a sufficient knowledge of Christ ?   Suppose we
yield the stories of the childhood, suppose we
admit — as indeed we must — that some of the
things recorded are questionable, it remains to
ask, Is it within the possible achievement of
criticism to obliterate the image of Christ presented in the Gospels?   The object of the Gospels is to preserve this image.   The picture
may be photographic, or it may be impression-
ist : in any case it is sufficient if it conveys to
us an idea of Jesus similar to that which His
associates received.   You do not put a Titian
or a Raphael or a Vandyke under the micro-
scope and pronounce the picture worthless when
you find a crack in the paint or a flaw in the
canvas ; you don't throw it aside as inaccurate
or misleading because a fold of the dress is in
bad drawing or because the painter has set a

jewel where it was never worn; neither is our esteem of the Gospels lessened by finding in their narrative events which perhaps never happened. The Gospels perfectly discharge their function if they present us with a Christ who is self-authenticating as the Revealer of God; if they show us how He claimed to be the Christ and how He made good this claim, if they reproduce a figure or personality which accounts for the Church and the Church's faith.

The reasons urged by criticism for our not accepting everything in the Gospels just as it stands are by no means groundless. On the contrary, they are such as cannot fail to emerge on sincere and thorough inquiry. The difficulties which one encounters may be distributed under four heads: (1) The general insecurity of oral tradition. (2) The tendency to admit what is mythical into the history of a hero and especially of the Christ. (3) The likelihood or possibility that the writers should allow their own opinions to color their statements. It has also (4) been observed that the three synoptists not infrequently disagree; and this is especially true of some of the more important parts of the narrative, such as that which recounts the resurrection.

Difficulties urged by criticism.

1. We must take into account the insecurity

of oral tradition and its liability in the course of years to become seriously adulterated. The circumstance that the Gospels were not written until nearly or quite a generation had elapsed since the events, and that during the interval the incidents of the life of Jesus had been orally handed down, can scarcely fail to have had some perceptible result in the character of the Gospels as we now have them. If the substance of them was the common property of the Christian Church during a whole generation, and if, during that period, every man was telling the story to his neighbor according to his own knowledge or fancy, if parents were crumbling the solid food for the use of their children, and preachers adapting the stories to the aptitudes of their audiences, is it not probable that the facts would come to be in some measure adulterated by fiction? As Orello Cone says: " That the tradition of Jesus, in the absence of a fixed and definite form, should have undergone no modification in passing through the media which it traversed before it was recorded in the Gospels, is incredible to any one who regards the conditions from an historical or psychological point of view."

This state of matters is at first sight alarming. But certain considerations reassure us.

(1) Too much may very easily be made of the distance in time between the events and their record. A second generation is sometimes spoken of as if it arrived all at once, and in a day displaced and abolished the first generation, like changing guard at a military post, or like the sudden displacement of day by night in the tropics. But many persons who had seen Jesus in Jerusalem and Galilee must have survived till the end of the century. Many must have been of an age to check the romancing of the evangelists, if such there was, by their own knowledge. And although our Gospels were not written till some considerable time had elapsed, their sources were probably current much earlier. Moreover, remoteness in time is often counterbalanced by the probability of the event and its congruity with the narrative of which it forms a part. The secular historian accepts testimony which has only come to light long after the event. Thus, in recording how Lady Nelson left the room when Nelson admiringly spoke of " dear Lady Hamilton," his biographer, Mahan, says, " Though committed to paper so many years later [in point of fact, forty-five] the incident is just one of those that stick to the memory and probably occurred substantially as told." And of an-

Record not contemporaneous with events.

other occurrence the same writer says, "This trifling incident, transpiring as it now does for the
first time, after nearly seventy years . . . bears
its own mute evidence." And the significant
utterance of Principal Drummond of Oxford is
here relevant: " If we suppose that the Synoptic Gospels were written from forty to sixty
years after the time of Christ, still they were
based on earlier material, and even after forty
years the memory of characteristic sayings may
be perfectly clear. . . . I have not a particularly
good memory, but I can recall many sayings
that were uttered forty or even fifty years ago,
and in some cases can vividly recollect the
scene."

*The Gospels
not mere
popular tra-
dition.*

(2) Another common error is to speak of our
Gospels as if, not being written till a generation after the events, they were, therefore, the
mere careless transcript of a popular tradition
adulterated by forty years of oral transmission,
and modified by the exigencies, idiosyncrasies,
and caprice of individual narrators. Whereas,
on the contrary, Luke expressly tells us that
he had made it his aim to get behind this popular tradition and to draw his narrative from
the original source, the eye-witnesses. Of
Mark's Gospel it is generally believed that
something similar may be said, and that it rep-

resents not the popular tradition, but the reminiscences of Peter. In other words, it is not to be assumed, as it so commonly is assumed, that because a Gospel is not written, say until the year 70 A.D., therefore, it is the transcript of the popular tradition of that period, the result of a generation of distortion and adulteration of history. On the contrary, it may be written for the very purpose of correcting such popular misconceptions.

(3) We must take into account the fact that one of our Gospels professes to be from the hand of an eye-witness. Of all means of ascertaining historical truth, the most satisfactory is the testimony of an eye-witness. An eye-witness may be confused, as in complicated political affairs or in a great battle ; he may be biassed, or his memory may be treacherous, or he may have in view some other end than that of merely recording what took place. But although an eye-witness may err, the presumption is always in his favor, and his account is received until proved erroneous. Thus — to make use again of the biography already alluded to — Mrs. St. George, mother of Archbishop Trench, records in her journal that on one occasion she saw Nelson under the influence of wine. And on this entry Nelson's

Value of eye-witness.

biographer remarks : " However much to be deplored, such an occurrence is not so impossible as to invalidate the testimony of an eyewitness, even in a man of Nelson's well-established habitual abstemiousness, which indeed his health necessitated."

Fourth evangelist claims to be eye-witness.

Now one of our Gospels expressly claims to be from the hand of one who saw and was a part of what he describes. In the fourth Gospel we not only find the sworn evidence of an eye-witness in regard to *one* astonishing circumstance, — the issuing of blood and water from the pierced side of the crucified, — " He that saw it bear record and his record is true ; " but the whole Gospel is vouched for as the work of an eye-witness by the appended note: " This [viz. the disciple whom Jesus loved] is the disciple who testifieth of these things *and wrote* these things, and we know that his testimony is true." For my own part I have not the audacity to disregard this express affirmation. Whether the order of events in this Gospel is the actual order, whether the discourses are recorded as delivered, what liberties have been taken with the material, these are other and subordinate questions ; but that those who first published the Gospel knew it to be from the hand of the Apostle

John, I have no doubt. *When* it was written, the date at which John began to put in writing that which filled his life, cannot be ascertained. Probably much of it was written long before its publication. But the inevitable meaning of the note is, that the Apostle John was not only the source or guarantor of the tradition which is perpetuated in the Gospel, but that he actually wrote it. The attempted evasions of this plain statement can scarcely be taken seriously.

As countervailing this express affirmation, or at any rate as obscuring the mode in which the material has been treated, there is of course much that must be taken into account. It is a different Christ that is here represented, it is said. But this is a difficulty decisively set aside by Christendom, which has always found it easy to form one consistent portrait from the four accounts. Or we are told that the author was a philosopher, not a fisherman. Would any one but a fisherman have told us the exact number of his catch, one hundred and fifty-three? Even Dr. Evelyn Abbott finds in this number mysterious allusions to the Church as evolved from the Law and the Spirit, and so forth. Did Dr. Abbott ever know of a fisherman who did not count his take and loudly proclaim its number if it was large?

Evidence substantiating his claim.

Who but a boatman would have given us
that complicated arrangement of boats in the
sixth chapter, to account for the transfer of our
Lord's audience from one side of the lake to
the other, a transfer for which there was no
possible necessity if the author was not writing
the fact as it happened, but freely inventing?

Memorable character of the events.

(4) When we allow for the lapse of time
between the events and their record, we must
also allow for the extraordinary and memorable
character of the material. The character of
Jesus, it will on all hands be admitted, was so
unique and impressive that even if His associates could not present the whole of it in all its
aspects, yet they were likely to retain very
clearly in their minds some main features of it.
Napoleon was a man of whom we have very
diverse details handed down to us by his officers
and members of his household and court, yet
the general impression he makes and the idea
commonly held of his character may be said to
be uniform. In the case of our Lord inadequate
representation was likely enough, erroneous representation not so likely. The same is true of
the most striking scenes and incidents of His
life. Such things make at once an ineffaceable
impression. Who that saw the paralytic let
down through the roof was at all likely to for-

get the scene? And, when the whole public life was of this striking kind and the death of so conspicuous and impressive a character, mistake was not so likely as with a commonplace, ordinary, uneventful existence.

But it is, as I have said, mainly the personality and general features of Christ and His ministry we need to know and seek to know, and the admitted impressiveness of this character must be taken into account. Dr. Abbott has been at great pains to illustrate the untrustworthiness of the Gospels from the untrustworthiness of the records of the life and death of Thomas à Becket. Some of these accounts were written within five years of his martyrdom, and many of the miracles recorded were set down in writing at the very time of their supposed occurrence, and yet there can be little doubt that, as Dr. Abbott says, "portentous falsehoods" have crept in, and that even eyewitnesses fall into astonishing errors. And Dr. Percy Gardner calls attention to the analogous fact that in the course of the half-century which followed the death of St. Francis of Assisi, "his legend went on growing and changing, forming round itself a larger and larger halo of supernatural power and glory, and adapting itself to the fortunes of the Franciscan Society."

Rapid growth of marvels.

Does not obscure impression made by character.

But these arguments only serve to bring out how powerless such legends are to dull the impression made by the man round whom they cling. Notwithstanding this accumulation of fictitious excrescence, the characters of Becket and of Francis stand out clearly. How much more is this the case with the transcendently powerful and impressive character of Jesus. The impression He made on those who companied with Him was unique, an impression not likely to be dulled by time, an impression made upon many.

Especially impression upon simple minds

Account must also be taken of the character and circumstances of those who received this impression. It is sometimes objected to them, as it was by the pedants of the Sanhedrin, that they were unlearned and ignorant men. But this very characteristic rendered them more susceptible of pure and unbiassed impression, an impression impossible or not so likely in men who already had definite opinions and prepossessions. They were the "babes," on the *tabula rasa* of whose open and uninscribed minds Jesus could imprint His influence.

unblurred by previous impressions.

As an eloquent writer has said: "With the man who lives a life full of bustling energy impression overlays impression, till all is blurred and confused. But in the life of a peasant impressions are so rare that they assume abnormal vividness; and thus a certain event or incident, which at the time seemed extraordinary, is an indelible spot of light in the gray gloom of many monotonous and narrow years. The men who saw most of Christ were of this order. The most thrilling hour they had ever known was that in which Christ first addressed them. In many cases their meeting with Christ had been associated with some tragic or impressive incident which they were not likely to forget — the threatened death of a parent, the recovery from sickness of a friend, the recall to sanity of a demented child. . . . The wings of wonder had hovered over the gray lives of these men for a day and a night, their hearts, their imaginations, had been strangely stirred. Was it likely that they could forget?"[1]

2. The known tendency to admit what is mythical into the account given of any hero naturally excites suspicion that something of the kind may have happened in the case of our Gospels. The narrative of Jesus ran the risk of being adulterated by the tendency to ascribe to Him every marvellous quality and action which had been ascribed to the heroes of the Old Testament; and especially to relate of

Mythical tendency.

[1] Dawson, " Life of Christ."

Jesus, as accomplished facts, all that the prophets had foretold of the Messiah. In the Old
Testament they found certain actions and attributes ascribed to the Messiah; Jesus was
the Messiah, therefore all those actions and
attributes must have been manifested by
Him.

Applied to Gospels.

This line of criticism and the material it
affords were thoroughly exploited, and with
consummate ability and knowledge, by Strauss.
And it maintains its hold on some of the foremost living critics. Holtzmann, for example,
maintains that although in details it may be
difficult always to lay one's finger on the Old
Testament reminiscence which reappears in the
Gospels, yet the support which a legendary
representation has in the events of the actual
life of Jesus can be shown. And Dr. Percy
Gardner, in his "Historic View of the New
Testament," has the following: "When the
first missionaries went to preach in the towns
of Judæa, the commonest objection which they
would meet to the proclamation of Jesus as the
Messiah would be that the life of the Master,
His birth, and His death did not conform to
the prophetic writings. How could the Messiah be born in Galilee? How could He fail to
be of the family of David? He must, like the

prophet of Isaiah, be silent in the presence of His accusers; He must, like the King in Zechariah, come riding upon an ass. His garments must have been seized and divided among His enemies, according to the words of the twenty-second Psalm. He must have made His grave with the rich, and so forth. Now by far the easiest way of meeting these objections would be to say, ' Exactly, thus it was with our Master.' And thus many tales, however arising, which possessed the great merit of bringing the life of Jesus into conformity with prophecy, would have a natural advantage which would insure their survival in the competition for existence, and which would secure them a place in the biographies accepted in the Society."

Now, in the first place, the limited range of this objection must be remarked. It is not doubted that in essentials Jesus more than fulfilled the anticipations of the prophets — that He was a Messiah of a spiritual grandeur far surpassing the picture we can compose from the scattered features drawn in the Old Testament. If any Evangelist was met by the supposed objection that Jesus did not correspond to the Old Testament picture, and if he yielded to the temptation to bring the reality into apparent harmony with the expectation, this

Applies only to petty details.

could only happen in relation to some of the insignificant externals and details.

And mainly among Jews.
It should also be remarked that this inducement to falsification could exist only in preaching to Jews, and, among them, to those who had made some study of the Messianic predictions. How variously these were interpreted is well known. The Gentile Church could at first have little interest in such points. That some Jews might ask, that some did ask, for a correspondence between Jesus and the prophecies regarding the Messiah is certain, but that an Evangelist would unscrupulously falsify facts, which might be quite as well known to the objector as to the preacher, is not so credible. For let us take the case selected by Dr. Gardner, the descent of the Messiah from David. We know that this was a main point in the identification of the Messiah, "Hath not the Scripture said, that Christ cometh of the seed of David, and out of the town of Bethlehem, where David was?" And the Evangelists met this demand, but how? Not by making a bare affirmation, unsupported by any evidence, that in this respect Jesus verified prediction, but by publishing his genealogy — a method which exposed them to final refutation if it was fictitious, for a

Jewish pedigree could be ascertained beyond question.

But the truth is, that there is no evidence that the first believers in general were greatly concerned about such matters. Even Paul, whom one might have expected to make a great point of such correspondences, rests his faith on much more central and essential matters. And if any credit is to be given to John's account of the manner in which the earliest disciples attached themselves to Jesus, we can recognize in it how little weight these correspondences had. "Can any good come out of Nazareth?" says the objector; and the answer is, "Come and see;" not as Dr. Gardner would have us believe, "He does not belong to Nazareth but to Bethlehem."

First believers not triflers.

3. We must take into account the likelihood that the writers would allow their own opinions to color their statements. By the time the Gospels were written many thorny questions had arisen in the Church, and men had taken their sides. Some quoted Jesus as supporting their opinion, while others held Him to have meant quite the opposite. It was not in human nature that a writer who had a strong view on some controverted point should compose a Gospel without letting it be seen to which

Are the Gospels partisan?

party he belonged.   Holtzmann positively says, "No evangelist writes history like Herodotus, merely to repeat what he had heard; they all pursue more or less some religious interest." The personal equation must be ascertained. As Oliver Wendell Holmes put it in chemical terms, "Smith gives you the Smithate of truth; Brown gives you the Brownate."

Reaction against this idea.   Little, however, need be said of this difficulty. At present its day would seem to be done and a reaction against it has set in. Thus, we find even Schmiedel saying that "on the whole, such tendencies as have been spoken of manifest themselves only in a few parts of the Gospels." Of course the different objects the evangelists had in view must have influenced their choice of material. Matthew, for example, omits features of various incidents which are carefully delineated in the other Gospels, because Matthew's constant aim is to get at the *sayings* of our Lord and put them on record. The language, too, of a writer is necessarily influenced by his temperament, education, and object; and such differences of this kind appear in the Gospels, as one would expect. But that the writers'. aims or predilections have seriously damaged the trustworthiness of the Gospels need not be suspected.

4. The discrepancies in the accounts which the Gospels give of the same event are supposed to invalidate their testimony. Thus, Schmiedel, in his article on the Resurrection in the "Encyclopædia Biblica," makes much use of this objection, and lays down the canon that discrepant accounts cannot be accepted in their main point of agreement unless this is confirmed from other sources. Regarding this argument, it is enough to quote, and it is a pleasure to quote the opinion of an unduly discredited author, whose strong Yorkshire sense would be invaluable at the present time. Paley says: "I know not a more rash or unphilosophical conduct of the understanding than to reject the substance of a story by reason of some diversity in the circumstances with which it is related. The usual character of human testimony is substantial truth under circumstantial variety. This is what the daily experience of courts of justice teaches. When accounts of a transaction come from the mouths of different witnesses, it is seldom that it is not possible to pick out apparent or real inconsistencies between them. These inconsistencies are studiously displayed by an adverse pleader, but oftentimes with little impression upon the minds of the judges. On the contrary, a close and minute agreement

Discrepancies.

induces the suspicion of confederacy and fraud.
When written histories touch upon the same
scenes of action, the comparison almost always
affords ground for a like reflection. Numerous
and sometimes important variations present
themselves; not seldom also, absolute and final
contradictions; yet neither the one nor the
other are deemed sufficient to shake the credibility of the main fact. The embassy of the
Jews to deprecate the execution of Claudius'
order to place his statue in their temple, Philo
places in harvest, Josephus in seedtime; both
contemporary writers. No reader is led by this
inconsistency to doubt whether such an order
was given. Our own history supplies examples
of the same kind. In the account of the Marquis of Argyll's death in the reign of Charles II,
we have a very remarkable contradiction. Lord
Clarendon relates that he was condemned to be
hanged, which was performed the same day;
on the contrary, Burnet, Wodrow, Heath, Ec-
hard, concur in stating that he was beheaded,
and that he was condemned upon the Saturday
and executed on a Monday. Was any reader
of English history ever sceptic enough to raise
from hence a question whether the Marquis of
Argyll was executed or not? Yet this ought
to be left in uncertainty, according to the prin-

ciples upon which the Christian history has sometimes been attacked."

But there are certain positive evidences of trustworthiness which must also be taken into account. *Positive evidence.*

(1) The sayings of Jesus have been preserved with remarkable accuracy. Some of them were of a self-preserving kind. They could not well be forgotten. They may have been dissevered from their original connection, but that is of less consequence. Strauss himself says : " The pithy sayings of Jesus could not, indeed, be dissolved by the flood of the oral tradition, but were, perhaps, not seldom torn from their natural connection, floated away from their original strata, and landed, like fragments of rock, in places where they do not really belong." Naturally the oral evangelist grouped together sayings that served his purpose, irrespective of the occasions on which they were spoken. In Matthew we have sayings culled from various scenes and occasions; but, as Renan with true literary sense remarks, there is in them an unmistakable ring which proves them to be the true product of the mind of Christ. *Sayings of Jesus accurately reported.*

No one can read the parables without feeling sure that they are genuine and accurately reported. The finish upon them, their family *In particular the parables.*

likeness in style and method, their aptness, all
testify to accuracy of report and exclude the
idea that they have been invented, tampered
with, or misrepresented by the evangelists.
How they have been so accurately reported is
something of a problem. But there they are;
and even Schmiedel seems to imply that they
are genuine. Dr. Percy Gardner indeed says,
"There are no entirely undisputed sayings of
Jesus." We might quite as truly say, "There
are no undisputed plays of Shakespeare," because some literary lunatic declares them to
have been the work of Bacon.

Retention of obsolete names. (2) A somewhat striking evidence of the
fidelity of the evangelists is to be found in their
retention of names and designations of our
Lord which had become obsolete in the second
generation. In that generation the name Jesus
had largely given place to the title Christ.
Christ had become the name of Him who bore
the office; but in the Gospels the regular name
used is Jesus. Similarly the designation "Son
of Man" was superseded in the second generation, but the evangelists, although never hear-
ing it used in their own day, preserved its use
by Jesus Himself. Other instances of a similar
fidelity might easily be adduced.

(3) Another sure evidence of the fidelity of

the Gospel narratives has usually and justly *Exposure of the failings of Apostles.* been found in their unhesitating and frank exposure of the weaknesses and failings of the Twelve; their slowness in apprehending the meaning of the parables, the failure of their faith on critical occasions, the worldliness of their ambitions, their wrangling with one another, their abandonment of the Lord in the hour of His need, all is frankly related. Nothing is hidden, nothing explained away, nothing excused. The thing as it happened is told, quite irrespective of the credit or discredit it reflected on this or that person. This characteristic of these narratives is of great importance, revealing as it does the objectivity of the narrative, the absence of personal considerations, the habit of mind which sees the thing as it is. Professor Fisher in his " Grounds of Theistic and Christian Belief," elaborates this argument and warrantably asks, " What surer mark of an honest narrative can exist than a willingness to give a plain unvarnished account of his own mortifying mistakes, and the consequent rebuffs, whether just or not, which he has experienced? When Boswell writes that Johnson said to him, with a stern look, ' Sir, I have known David Garrick longer than you have done, and I know no right you have to talk to me on the subject,' or, when an author tells us that his hero said to him, ' Sir, endeavor to clear your mind of cant,' no one can doubt that the biographer is telling a true story. Men are not likely to invent anecdotes to their own discredit. When we find them in any author, a strong presumption is raised in favor of his general truthfulness."

External attestation by Paul.
The strongest *external* attestation of the truthfulness of the Gospel representation of Jesus is that which is furnished by the letters of Paul. It is very questionable whether Paul ever saw any of our Gospels. Certainly he had not seen any of them prior to the formation of his own belief. But it is the same Christ we find in his letters. Here is the same person recognized as the Christ, the same perfectness of human character, the same underlying Divinity, the same death and resurrection. If Paul *had* known Christ through the Gospels, we do not know what alteration that could have made. The real Christ who appeared to him, and whom he learned to know by his own experience and by conversation with those who had known our Lord on earth, is in no respect different from the Christ of the Gospels. In short, the Christ we find in the Gospels is the Christ who won the faith and devotion of those

who knew Him at first hand, and upon whom, as its foundation, the Church was founded. The picture we have here is not a replica touched up by a painter of a later generation who has ideas of his own as to the expression of the features; it is the original painting which satisfied the personal friends of the subject.

Obviously, then, the critic cannot accept all and everything he finds recorded in the Gospels, but must possess himself of some touchstone by which all excrescence may be eliminated and the fact remain. This of course applies to the sayings of Jesus as much as to the events recorded. Where the synoptists present different forms of our Lord's sayings, it is sometimes as difficult as it is important to determine which is genuine. *A touchstone required.*

What, then, is the touchstone? Schmiedel's article in the "Encyclopædia Biblica" may be accepted as the high water mark of the criticism that claims to be scientific; and one satisfactory feature of that article is that it attempts to furnish us with a criterion by which we may sift the credible from the incredible in the Gospels. The criterion is thus stated : " When a profane historian finds before him a historical document which testifies to the worship of a hero *Schmiedel's touchstone.*

unknown to other sources, he attaches first and foremost importance to those features which cannot be deduced merely from the fact of this worship, and he does so on the simple and sufficient ground that they would not be found in this source unless the author had met with them as fixed data of tradition. . . . If we discover any such points, — even if only a few, — they guarantee not only their own contents, but also much more. For in that case one may also hold as credible all else which agrees in character with these, and is, in other respects, not open to suspicion. Indeed, the thoroughly disinterested historian must recognize it as his duty to investigate the grounds for this so great reverence for Himself which Jesus was able to call forth; and he will then, first and foremost, find himself led to recognize as true the two great facts that Jesus had compassion for the multitude and that He preached with power, not as the Scribes." The meagre results yielded by his criterion might well have provoked a reëxamination of its merits. The fact is, Schmiedel starves himself for fear of being poisoned. He throws away the baby with the dirty water of the bath. The founder of the Christian Church he finds to have been a benevolent person who was also a good preacher; a combination of Howard and White-field.

Not only do the results reflect discredit on this criterion, but its inherent incompetency is apparent. To put aside all the elements in the record which can be deduced from the fact of the hero's worship is to put aside all that is essential and to begin at the wrong end. Apply the principle to any other hero. At Nelson's death the nation sang: " His body is buried in peace, but his name liveth for evermore." In order to ascertain why his name thus lives, Schmiedel would, I presume, direct us to the facts that Nelson was vain and easily flattered, that he was carried off his feet by the blandishments of Lady Hamilton, that he was always ill when he went to sea — how far will these non-heroic facts carry us to the Nile and Trafalgar? Is it not obvious that we must begin with the facts which can account for the worship? *Its incompe-tence.*

Here, I think, we find our proper starting-point for the criticism of the Gospels and the true criterion of their credibility. We find in them that which alone explains the Christian Church; the one key which fits the lock. Do the Gospels set before us a self-authenticating Revealer of God? It is in the fact that Jesus *The true criterion.*

claimed to be the Christ, the representative of
God on earth, and justified this claim by giving
us in His life, death, and resurrection, a *self-
authenticating* revelation of God, — it is in this
fact that the Church finds its explanation, and
it is this figure, the figure of the Christ, that
the Gospels present.   Whatever fits this claim
and is congruous with it is credible.   The testimony of an eye-witness is only accepted when
he relates what is credible : and the testimony
of one who is removed by half a century from
the event he relates, may yet be accepted as
trustworthy if the incident he relates is congruous with what we otherwise know of the
person involved.   So that credibility is the
touchstone of testimony; and of credibility
itself, the criterion is congruity with what is
otherwise known.   Things that would never
be disputed if related of one person, will be
doubted and contested if told of another.   And
in the claim of Jesus to be the Christ, and His
acceptance as such by the disciples and the
Church, we have the criterion by which the
Gospels must be judged.   It is this central fact
which enables us to believe what they tell us of
His miracles and His resurrection.   If Jesus
was the representative of God on earth, if He
authenticates Himself as such, we may expect

unique incidents and much that is beyond
the ordinary reach of man. Particular manifestations may be doubted by this or that individual, but in the Messiahship there is laid a
ground for belief in the main tenor of the life
as related in the Gospels. We can believe of
this person, the Christ, what we could not believe of any other.

Here, then, we return to the question as
stated in the outset, Do the Gospels set before
us a credible Christ? Is the figure they depict
a true representation of the Christ? That it is
so in essentials cannot be questioned. The
figure presented in the Gospels is self-verifying
as God's representative. A revelation of God
superior to every other is made by the person
and ministry depicted. In these records we
find the best and highest we know — in a word,
God manifest in the flesh. *The Christ of the Gospels self-authenticating.*

No doubt it may still be objected that this
figure was the creation of the disciples, and
never really existed. That objection was ex-
ploded as long ago as Rousseau; and Ullmann,
in his criticism of Strauss, may be said to have
finally disposed of the alternative, Did the
Church create Christ? or did Christ create the Church? A figure so wholly dis-
appointing current Messianic expectation, so *Was He the creation of the evange-lists?*

traversing the ideas of good Jews that even the
Baptist misunderstood Him, could not be the
invention of a few peasants.   It suffices to cite
John Stuart Mill, who says: [1] " It is of no use
to say that Christ, as exhibited in the Gospels,
is not historical — who among His disciples or
among their proselytes was capable of inventing the sayings ascribed to Jesus, or of imagin-
ing the life and character revealed in the
Gospels?   Certainly not the fishermen of Galilee, as certainly not St. Paul."

Essential claims of Christ made good.   The grand essential characteristics of out-
standing individuals are understood by the
people, even though their birth or the particulars of their career are little known.   Clive
is recognized as having laid the foundations of
the British Indian Empire, Wellington as having broken the power of Napoleon, Watt as the
developer of the steam engine.   That Jesus was
the Christ was also recognized, and His rejection
and crucifixion by the authorities testify to His
claim.   The details by means of which this
claim was made and justified will be viewed
variously by various minds, but the claim is so
unique and marvellous that it discounts all sur-
prise at particular marvels which are recorded.

Conclusion.   What, then, may we reasonably conclude from

[1] " Essays," p. 233.

all this? It is not possible to say of the Gospels, "Everything herein recorded happened precisely as related." This is impossible for the simple reason that in some instances the several Gospels give us discrepant and irreconcilable accounts of the same event. Some events, such as the Virgin-birth, depend for their acceptance so largely upon preconceptions and the mental attitude of the reader, that it may be impossible to adduce convincing evidence of their truth. Of other narratives, such as that of the Gadarene demoniac, it may be felt that there is either some misunderstanding of what actually took place or some link omitted whose presence might have shed light on the incident. But such difficulties, omissions, and discrepancies cannot be said to alter or even to dim the central figure. It matters nothing so far as our preception of Christ and our belief in Him is concerned, whether He healed two blind men in Jericho or only one, nor whether this healing took place at His entrance to the city or His exit from it. *What is it we seek in the Gospels?* It is the knowledge of Christ. That the Gospels present us with a lifelike portrait of Christ and with so accurate a report of His words that we can form a true estimate of His teaching, this is not to be doubted. It is the Christ *of the Gospels* that has won the heart of Christendom and that in millions of instances has been found true and efficacious in the bringing of many sons to glory and to God. And from that majestic figure we must not allow our minds to be drawn aside by the minutiæ of criticism. The danger of criticism is not in what it discovers but in turning the mind aside to details and externals. Those who work in it tend to lose perspective and atmosphere. The warning of Amiel in another sphere is applicable to this: "There is a way of killing truth by truths. Under the pretence that we want to study it more in detail we pulverize the statue. It is an absurdity of which our pedantry is constantly guilty." [1]

[1] "Journal," II., 258.

VII

THE MIRACULOUS ELEMENT IN
THE GOSPELS

THE MIRACULOUS ELEMENT IN THE GOSPELS

THAT Jesus considered the healing of disease an important, or even an essential, feature of His work, is apparent both from His practice and from His words. His practice again and again elicits from the evangelists the remark that they are unable to record every individual cure. They content themselves with such summaries as we find in Luke iv. 40, "All they that had any sick with divers diseases brought them unto Him; and He laid His hands on every one of them, and healed them." The prominence which these physical cures had in His ministry is convincingly reflected in His fear lest the Messianic function should come to be identified with this form of ministry. And yet He found Himself constrained more than once to draw attention to His works of healing and to their significance. When Herod's threat was reported to Him, He almost gave the impression that His whole

The healing of disease essential to the work of Jesus.

213

work was to heal: "I will *perform cures* to-day
and to-morrow: and the third day I will be
perfected." Still more significant is His explanation of His reason, or one of His reasons, for
exorcism, which may be reckoned among His
works of healing. His justification is, that
the strong man armed who guards his own
house, — that is, Satan, — must be bound if
the contents of his house are to be spoiled.
The casting out of the devils was the binding
of the strong man, the necessary preliminary
to the taking possession of the Spirit of man
and the abolition of all Satanic results therein.
It was the sign that the kingdom, or reign
of God, had really begun among men (Luke
ii. 20).

Disparage-
ment of
miracle,

At the present time, however, the idea very
commonly obtains that Christianity would float
more buoyantly and prosperously were the
miraculous element in the Gospel narrative
thrown overboard. Men favorable to Christianity and of weighty mental caliber disparage
miracle, and deny that it is needed. Matthew
Arnold goes so far as to say,[1] "There is nothing one would more desire for a person or a
document one greatly values than to make them
independent of miracles." Harnack, the most

[1] " Literature and Dogma," p. 137.

prominent of living German critics, recently undertook to tell the world what was "the essence of Christianity," and he definitely excludes the miraculous: "We must either decide to rest our belief on a foundation unstable and always exposed to fresh doubts or else we must abandon this foundation altogether, and with it the miraculous appeal to our senses." And again : "We are firmly convinced that what happens in space and time is subject to the general laws of motion, and that in this sense, as an interruption of the order of nature, there can be no such thing as miracle."

It is not only professed sceptics who in our *even by* time assume this attitude of distrust or sus- *apologists.* pended judgment toward the miraculous. Defenders of the faith manifest the same uneasiness. Dr. Rashdall, certainly one of the ablest living philosophical theists, while maintaining that the visions of our Lord after the resurrection "were not mere subjective delusions," yet expresses himself strongly in regard to the miraculous. "We may be quite confident," he says, "that for minds which have once appreciated the principles of historical criticism, or minds affected by the diffused scepticism which has sprung from historical criticism, neither religious faith in general

nor any doctrine of primary religious importance, will ever depend mainly upon the evidence of abnormal events recorded to have
happened in the remote past."[1]

But it is needless accumulating testimonies.
Every one is already aware that the idea very
widely prevails that the Gospel miracles are an
excrescence marring the simplicity and beauty
of the life of our Lord, and that if once they
served a purpose, which is very doubtful, it
were better now to say nothing about them.
Thus Browning compares them to the dry twigs
stuck round a newly sown flower-plot to preserve it from the trampling beasts, but when
the plants themselves are grown, visible, strong,
overtopping the hedge, the preserving sticks
are thrown into the rubbish heap.

Miracles an incubus while mis-understood.   The ethics of Christianity, it is supposed, if cut
free from this incubus, would assert their supe-
riority and attract all men.   And of course so
long as the miracles of our Lord are not recognized as an essential part of His revelation, so
long will they be felt to be a hindrance and not
a help to faith.   But Jesus evidently considered miraculous works of healing an essential
element in His work, and whoever feels uneasy
about the miraculous, and fancies that perhaps

[1] " Contentio Veritatis," p. 58.

it would be well to yield the point and surrender miracle, must be looking at the matter with very different eyes from those with which our Lord viewed it. Hence the importance of considering His attitude toward miracle.

It has recently been most pertinently asked : "If it was worth Christ's while in His short earthly life to fatigue Himself in physical miracles of healing, is it not worth our while to attend to the fact, to be grateful for it, and to hand on to others, undiminished, the full record of His gracious help to human need, and of His manifold appeal to human faith?"[1]

The points which seem especially to demand consideration at present are these : What precisely we claim for Jesus in claiming the power to work miracles. Is it merely faith-healing or some greater power? What importance and significance did Jesus Himself attach to the working of miracles, and in what relation did they stand to the whole of His work of revealing the Father? After considering these points, we may take up one or two of the common objections. *Points demanding consideration.*

1. First, then, the Gospels claim for Jesus some greater power than that of healing the sick — some power which they called and which *Terms denoting miracle.*

[1] Mackintosh, "Apologetics," p. 48.

we also call miraculous. There is little need
that we lay down any hard-and-fast definition
of miracle. But one or two words of explanation are perhaps necessary at the outset. In
the New Testament we find four words applied
to the same phenomenon, marvel, sign, work,
power. Our word "miracle" corresponds only
to the first of these, and therefore leaves out of
view three-fourths of the characteristics of the
phenomenon. It is not only a marvel calling
men's attention, "ringing the bell of the universe," as John Foster said ; it also responds to
the attention and inquiry aroused by being a
"sign," revealing a spiritual presence, or em-
bodying and illustrating a spiritual truth ; it is
also preëminently a "work" advancing some
beneficent and worthy object and fitting itself
in as an essential part of the task given Him
by the Father to do. It is, besides, a "power,"
transcending ordinary human endeavor and
bringing to bear on human affairs and for the
relief of human needs a force of irresistible
might.[1]

*Explana-
tions of mir-
acle.*

These are the features of miracle which
should be presented to the mind when we
speak of the miracles of Jesus. Sometimes we

[1] Cf. Lyman Abbott's "Theology of an Evolutionist,"
p. 134.

know a thing better when we do not try to define it. But if definitions are wanted, they can be found in abundance in Chapuis' " Du Surnaturel," or in Trench, or Mozley, or in Pfleiderer's "Philosophy of Religion." There are two explanations of miracle which are interesting : that which explains it as the introduction of a higher and to us unfamiliar law, and that which refers it to the immediate action of the Divine will. Of the former explanation Carlyle in his " Sartor " may be taken as the exponent. " But is not a real miracle simply a violation of the Laws of Nature ? ask several. Whom I answer by this new question, What are the Laws of Nature ? To me perhaps the rising from the dead were no violation of these Laws, but a confirmation, were some far deeper law now first penetrated into, and by Spiritual Force, even as the rest have all been, brought to bear on us with its Material Force." But this supposition, although it finds much to support it, remains an unverified, and by the nature of the case unverifiable, hypothesis.

The reference of miracle to the direct action *Referable to* of the Divine will is the most straightforward *the Divine will* explanation. In ourselves we have before us the constant proof that spirit acts directly upon matter : our will, invisible, intangible, spiritual,

moves our hands, feet, and other organs — *how*
we do not know. But here we see spirit act-
ing directly on matter; and, instructed by this
experience, we seem to find it not inconceivable
that the Divine will should be so intimate to
the material world as to act directly upon it
and accomplish results which without the intervention of that will would not have taken place.

and wrought by faith. Now our Lord claims that the miracles He
performed were the works given Him by the
Father to do. They were done, no doubt,
through His own will, but there was behind
it the Divine will. And therefore He declared
that the power of working miracles was within
reach of every one who believed in God.
When the disciples asked Him why they were
unable to heal a lunatic boy, His answer was,
"Because of your unbelief, for verily I say
unto you, If ye have faith as a grain of mustard
seed, ye shall say unto this mountain, Remove
hence to yonder place, and it shall remove, and
nothing shall be impossible unto you." Peter
is assured that he also could have walked on
the water had he had sufficient faith. It was
not on an independent power of His own nor
on the magic of His own personality our Lord
depended, but on His closeness to the Father.
Just as He rebuked the young man who

ascribed to Him independent goodness, so would He say of His miracles, There is none *mighty* but God.

It is important to observe this reference by our Lord to the will of the Father, because it differentiates Him from the mere hypnotist or faith-healer. That many of our Lord's cures may legitimately be classed with the ordinary manifestations of faith-healing is not to be denied. It is needless in our day to insist upon the reality of such manifestations, because science has taken up a line of inquiry which puts them beyond question and at the same time explains their nature. In Tuke's "Illustrations of the Influence of the Mind upon the Body in Health and Disease," or in Carpenter's "Mental Physiology," or in Alice Fielding's "Faith-healing and Christian Science," sufficient evidence is cited to show that one of the most potent agents in dispelling certain forms of disease is confident expectation of cure. Thus Dr. Carpenter in his authoritative work states : "That the confident expectation of a cure is the most potent means of bringing it about, doing that which no medical treatment can accomplish, may be affirmed as the generalized result of experiences of the most varied kind, extending through a long

Faith-healing.

series of ages. . . . For although there can
be no doubt that in a great number of cases
the patients have *believed themselves* to be
cured, when no *real amelioration* of their condition had taken place, yet there is a large
body of trustworthy evidence, that permanent
amendment of a kind perfectly obvious to
others has shown itself in a great variety of
local maladies, when the patients have been
sufficiently possessed by the *expectation* of benefit and by *faith* in the efficacy of the means
employed."

Faith-cures genuine.

The certification, by medical science and
psychological observation, of the genuineness
of cures wrought by the expectation of cure,
has been eagerly accepted by many as giving
all the explanation required of the miracles of
Christ. Those cures were actually performed
and gave the suggestion and the ground of the
ascription of other and greater miracles. Although those cures are now explained in conformity with well-ascertained natural laws, yet
in the time of our Lord they were supposed to
be miraculous, and once the door was opened to
miracle, crowds entered without the legitimate
pass. Certainly this explanation will occur to
any thoughtful mind.

Our reasons for being dissatisfied with it are

(1) that while in some respects the cures ac- *Differenti-*
complished by Jesus resembled those of the *ated from*
miracles.
hypnotist or faith-healer, in other respects they
differed. They resembled them in always re-
quiring faith in the patient. Where there was
no faith our Lord *could* do no mighty works.
Sometimes, that faith seems to have been a mere
expectation to be healed, a vague, superstitious,
ignorant expectation. But the faith of the
patient was not recognized by our Lord as the
sole or even the main factor in the cure. His
own faith was always directed toward the supreme will. He prayed before raising Lazarus.
He declares that certain kinds of exorcism can
only be achieved by prayer. On the one hand
He brought Himself into so living a sympathy
with the sufferer that it could be said that " He
took our infirmities and bore our sicknesses,"
while on the other hand He became the pure
channel of the Father's will. It was not by a
mere wave of the hand or utterance of a formula the cure was accomplished, but only by
putting Himself in the place of the sufferer on
the one hand and by being in the purest and
most absolute harmony with God on the other
hand.

It may no doubt be said that our Lord was
mistaken in supposing that the special will of

God had anything to do with the cures; that they were instances of the ordinary law, that expectation of a cure, irrespective of any special intervention of God, works wonders in certain forms of nervous disorders. We should, I think, be slow to ascribe such ignorance to our Lord; but, in any case, the fact remains that He was conscious of being in harmony with God, and thus in His hands these works became the expression of the Father's good will to men.

Miracles of Jesus not exclusively cures of nervous disorders,

But (2) besides this, cures of nervous disorders were not the only form in which Christ's power of working miracle was manifested. His ministry was characterized further by healings of leprosy, fever, and other maladies, by healing at a distance where no physical contact was possible, even by raisings from the dead, and by remarkable manifestations of power over nature. And undoubtedly the proof of these will depend not upon our knowledge of the similarity of the powers of Jesus to those of ordinary men, but upon the conception we entertain of that which distinguished Him from others. If we accept Him as the Christ and believe in His unbroken and perfect union with God, we shall be prepared to admit that exceptional manifestations may be expected in His career.

(3) It is further to be observed that the *nor exclu-* miracles which exhibit power over nature come *sively works of healing.* to us on the very same documentary evidence as the miracles of healing. This does not compel belief, but it requires that the introduction of such occurrences into the Gospels should be accounted for. Generally it is accounted for by the assertion that these accounts were the reflection of the opinion of those of the second Christian generation in whose time they were written. But unfortunately for this hypothesis, remarkably little account was made of Christ's miracles in that generation. Neither in the Epistles of Paul, nor in the Acts, are they alluded to more than once or twice. And, as Dr. Chase has pointed out, this constitutes " a strong historical argument against the position that in the days when the Gospels were written there was a tendency at work among the disciples which impelled them to decorate the story of their Master's life with fictitious miracles." [1]

But if we are to accept miracle, we must first *Function of* recognize its true function and significance — *miracle.* the relation it holds to the entire work of Christ. What, then, was our Lord's purpose in performing miracles? The answer is, He

[1] "Supernatural Element," p. 16.

performed them not to convince people that
He was the Messiah, the messenger and representative of God, but because He had that
understanding of God's love and that perfect
fellowship with God which made Him the
Messiah.

*Not to con-
vince men
of His Mes-
siahship,*

*He wrought no miracle for the purpose of con-
vincing men of His Messiahship.* From the first,
indeed, this constituted one of His typical, normal temptations. The people expected that by
some stupendous sign, such as leaping from the
temple roof, and alighting unhurt in the court
below, the Messiah would declare Himself. But
any such sign wholly disconnected from the
spiritual character of His work He resolutely,
peremptorily, and persistently refused. Nor
were any of the wonderful works He did done
for the purpose of persuading men. Their
primary purpose was to relieve distress. He
came to proclaim and establish God's Kingdom
among men, to *manifest God's presence and love.*
This He did more effectually by His works of
healing than by His teaching. It was His miracles that impressed men with a sense of the
Divine compassion; they were the revelation
of the Father's sympathy. Disease, Christ felt,
is incongruous with the Kingdom of God; and
if he is to exhibit that Kingdom, it must be

manifested in the physical as in the spiritual sphere. He was grieved when confronted with disease and death. This, He felt, is not the world as the Father would have it and means it to be. In so far as He had power to remove the distresses of men, He felt called upon to do so. Those healings were the works given Him by the Father to do. They manifested God's love because done out of pure compassion in the Father's name and with the Father's power. As it was by the power of God He achieved those cures, so it was the love of God that prompted them; and therefore He could say, " If I by the finger of God cast out devils, then is the *Kingdom of God* come unto you." These were the works congruous to God's presence, and accomplishing results which exhibited the Kingdom.

But just because the primary purpose of the *yet did con-* miracles was to give expression to God's mercy *vince men.* and not to prove our Lord's Messiahship, on this very account they can be appealed to as evidence that Jesus was the Messiah. The poet writes because he is a poet, and not for the purpose of convincing the world that he is a poet. And yet his writing does convince the world that he is a poet. The benevolent man acts precisely as Christ did when He laid His finger on the lips of the healed person and charged him to make no mention of His kindness, and therefore all who do come to the knowledge of it recognize him as a charitable person. Actions done for the purpose of establishing a character for courage or compassion or what not, are much more likely to establish a character for vanity and love of display. And it is just because the *primary* intention of Christ's miracles was not to establish a character for this or that, but directly to help needy persons, and so give utterance to God's love, that they do convincingly prove Him to be God's representative, the true King of the new Kingdom. Accordingly Jesus does not scruple on occasion to appeal to His miracles: "The works which the Father hath given me to finish, the same works that I do, bear witness of me, that the Father hath sent me;" and again, "Though ye believe not me, believe the works."

What the true "signs" are. St. Matthew records (xvi. 1–4) a significant conversation between our Lord and the combined Sadducees and Pharisees on this point. They came to Him with their usual demand for a convincing sign from heaven, continuing thus the initial temptation to end all dubiety about His Messianic dignity by some astounding feat or outward display. To this appeal He replies:

"In the evening ye say, It will be fair weather, for the sky is red : and in the morning, There will be a storm to-day, for it is lowering red. Ye know how to read the face of the sky, and can ye not read the signs of the times ? " You know the sequences of nature, and understand that certain results uniformly follow certain appearances. But you have no eye for spiritual sequences. You do not recognize that a clever feat, or a supernatural marvel which makes men stare, has no natural relation to the bless-ings of the Messianic Kingdom. Neither do you perceive that the presence among you of One in perfect harmony with God and devoted to human interests must result in a kind of weather altogether new in the spiritual world. You do not see that the entrance into the world of perfect humanity, of God in human form, applying Himself with all His Divine love and power to the actual needs of men, portends more good to the race than the greatest physical marvel could suggest. Suppose I did clothe the sun with a cloud as ye gaze upon it in the bare heavens ; suppose I commanded those mountains to be removed, or leapt unhurt from the temple roof to the courts below, there is no necessary and infallible connection between such marvels and the establishment of God's

Kingdom among men or their deliverance from
sin. You could not from your observation of
such phenomena predict what would result ;
but if you could read the signs of the times,
you might infallibly argue that One in perfect
accord with God could not enter into this
world's life and become a part of its history
without setting in motion a train of never-
ending and infinitely beneficent consequences.

The mira-
cles as
signs.
Very markedly and repeatedly in the fourth
Gospel is the faith that is quickened by a sense
of the personal majesty of Jesus shown to be
more trustworthy than a faith founded on His
miracles. But we must not on that account
deny any virtue to miracles in creating faith.
As our Lord Himself told Nicodemus, the Kingdom of God is a spiritual thing, and could only
be spiritually discerned by those who are born
of the spirit. Those only could enter it who
were attracted to Him by spiritual affinities.
His claims were recognized by those who had
eyes to see them, that is, by those who could
appreciate Divine goodness, the glory that con-
sisted in humiliation and in being the servant
of all. But the miracles served as object-les-
sons for those who were not in the front rank
of the spiritually sensitive. His power to give
the blind their sight suggested God's desire to

remove spiritual blindness; His feeding the hungry was His way of saying, Your Father suffers with you and cannot see you want. His strengthening of the impotent man plainly said, I will that you have eternal life and vitality. They were, in short, a prominent, important, and legible part of the revelation of the Father made by Christ.

It is, then, to misunderstand Christ's own conception of His miracles and their function, either, on the one hand, to suppose that their main function was evidential, or, on the other hand, to suppose that they have no evidential function. To consider them an obstacle rather than a help to faith is to misconceive the situation. The fact that they occupy so large a part in the narrative, and so large a part in the life of Christ is proof enough that they served an important purpose. That purpose was to bring the love of the Father into contact with the woes of men. They were the greatest means, second to the Cross, of manifesting God's love.

Revealing function of miracles.

The objections which at present are brought against the Gospel miracles are chiefly two, — that they cannot be proved, and that they are useless even though proved.

The apparently weightier objection that miracles are impossible is not now urged. The

Are miracles possible?

position of those who refuse to accept miracle
has shifted since the time when Spinoza could
say, "A miracle, whether contrary to, or above
nature, is a sheer absurdity." The argument
which led him to this conclusion is interesting
and enlightening. It was this : "Nothing happens in nature which does not follow from its
laws; these laws extend to all which enters the
Divine mind; and, lastly, nature proceeds in a
fixed and changeless course—whence it follows
that the word 'Miracle' can only be understood
in relation to the opinions of mankind, and signifies nothing more than an event, a phenomenon, the cause of which cannot be explained by
another familiar instance. . . . I might say,
indeed, that a miracle was *that*, the cause of
which cannot be explained by our natural understanding from the known principles of natural things." The core of this argument is the
same as that which lingers in some scientific
schools; viz., that as all nature with its laws is
the expression of the Divine mind, if anything
happens contrary to these laws, this must be
repugnant to the will of God. But obviously
this position of Spinoza's is a *petitio principii*,
—it takes for granted the main question, Is
the whole will of God expressed in nature?
In fact, this argument of Spinoza's leads us to

see that the question of the possibility of miracle is really the question, Is God supernatural?
Granting that the Divine life is immanent in
all nature, is there also a transcendent will
which is not bound by nature's laws, but can
assert itself on occasion irrespective of them?
In other words, Is God identified with nature,
or is He different from and superior to it?

But this position of Spinoza's is generally *Huxley's
definition of
impossibil-
ity.*
departed from. And no one has more decisively pronounced against it than Professor
Huxley. "Strictly speaking," he says, "I am
unaware of anything that has a right to the
title of an 'impossibility,' except a contradiction in terms. There are impossibilities logical,
but none natural. A 'round square,' a 'present past,' 'two parallel lines that intersect,' are
impossibilities, because the ideas denoted by
the predicates, 'round,' 'present,' 'intersect,'
are contradictory of the ideas denoted by the
subjects, 'square,' 'past,' 'parallel.' But walk-
ing on water, or turning water into wine, or
procreation without male intervention, or raising the dead, are plainly not 'impossibilities,'
in this sense." It might be otherwise, he goes
on to say, if our present knowledge of nature
exhausted the possibilities of nature, "but it is
sufficiently obvious not only that we are at the

beginning of our knowledge of nature, instead
of having arrived at the end of it, but that the
limitations of our faculties are such that we
never can be in a position to set bounds to the
possibilities of nature.　We have knowledge of
what is happening and what has happened ; of
what will happen we have and can have no
more than expectation, grounded on our more
or less correct reading of past experience, and
prompted by the faith begotten of that experience, that the order of nature in the future will
resemble its order in the past." In this remarkable passage Huxley is careful to exclude
the Divine Will, and thus virtually excludes
what is implied in the Gospel miracles.　Nature may have surprises for us, but we must
be guided in our expectations by our experience of her uniformity.　In short, he is so sure
of the impossibility of proving the occurrence
of what is contrary to natural law, that he does
not feel called upon to deny the possibility of
such phenomena.

*Impossibil-
ity of proof.*　It is, then, the impossibility of proof rather
than the *a priori* impossibility of miracle which
is now urged.　This received its classical expression from Hume in the often cited words :
"There is not to be found in all history, any
miracle attested by a sufficient number of men,

of such unquestioned goodness, education, and learning as to secure us against all delusion in themselves; of such undoubted integrity as to place them beyond all suspicion of any design to deceive others; of such credit and reputation in the eyes of mankind as to have a great deal to lose in case of their being detected in any falsehood; and at the same time, attesting facts performed in such a public manner, and in so celebrated a part of the world, as to render the detection unavoidable; all which circumstances are requisite to give us a full assurance in the testimony of men." How far this attitude toward the Gospel miracles has gained upon thoroughly Christian critics may be gathered from the very able statement of the matter which is given by Dr. Rashdall in " Contentio Veritatis,"[1] and in which the following occurs: " The idea of a suspension of natural law is not *a priori* inadmissible. At the same time, since such an admission would destroy all the criteria, both of scientific and historical reasoning, the admission of such a suspension could not reasonably be accepted without an amount of evidence which is practically unattainable in reference to the events of the distant past." This sense of the extreme difficulty

[1] p. 56.

of finding sufficient evidence to establish any breach of the uniformity of nature in the past, has been, I need scarcely say, enormously reënforced in recent years by the extended knowledge of natural law, and the increased sensitiveness to the uniformity of nature which results from the dominance of scientific research, as well as by the more exact study of history which has vastly increased the perception of the kind and amount of evidence required to establish any supposed occurrence.

Comparative study of miracles.

Together with this, the study of history has also enabled us to pursue the *comparative* study of miracles. Many sincere inquirers cordially accept Matthew Arnold's words: "The time has come when the minds of men no longer put as a matter of course the Bible miracles in a class by themselves. Now, from the moment this time commences, from the moment that the comparative history of all miracles is a conception entertained and a study admitted, the conclusion is certain, the reign of the Bible miracles is doomed."[1] This comparative study of miracles has been zealously pursued, and it has been shown that supernatural powers have been freely ascribed to the Buddha and the Bab, to Thomas à Becket and St. Francis of

[1] "God and the Bible," p. 46.

Assisi. The miracles of Jesus are supposed to be so analogous to those of other founders and saints that if we reject the one we are bound to reject the other. Thus Mr. Percy Gardner, in his instructive "Historic View of the New Testament,"[1] says: "Whether we investigate the history of the past or turn our attention to the less civilized countries of the world in which we live, we find that no class of phenomena is a more constant concomitant of the story of the rise and progress of religions than the miraculous; that a prophet will scarcely be listened to in any land unless he is credited by his followers with the power of reversing or superseding the laws of nature; that marvels follow the steps of the saint by an inevitable law of human nature." Similarly, Professor Carpenter, in "The Bible of the Nineteenth Century,"[2] puts forward the same plea: "The truth is," he says, "that the studies of the last generation have brought to light a wide range of facts showing that from the lowest forms of savage cults up to the more refined beliefs of the higher religions the presence of the miraculous is invariable."

Here, then, we are confronted with two difficulties, neither of which is a vamped up

Conditions of credibility.

[1] p. 147.   [2] p. 358.

objection, but on the contrary it is what will
inevitably occur to every one who is trying to
find a reasonable faith. The miracles ascribed
to Jesus are violations of the uniformity of
nature as known to us, and miracles are very
commonly ascribed to the founders and saints
of religions. I think both these difficulties are
removed if we take into account the *occasion*,
the *nature*, and the *worker* of the Gospel miracles. We may legitimately ask for stronger
evidence for a miracle so stupendous as the
standing still of the sun, the *occasion* being
merely to make a defeat more crushing. We
may feel we have not sufficient evidence to
enable us cordially to accept that astounding
miracle recorded by Matthew of the dead bodies
of the saints coming out of their tombs apparently to accomplish nothing. But the miracles
of healing and even the miracle of the resurrection do not seem incredible when we consider the greatness of the occasion, the character
of the miracles in question, and especially the
uniqueness of Him who wrought them.

Huxley's challenge. This will be more evident if we accept Huxley's challenge and choose a concrete instance
with which to compare the Gospel miracles.
He asks in a somewhat triumphant tone if any
testimony would suffice to make it credible

that a centaur had been seen trotting down
Regent Street. The instance selected does not
show Huxley's usual sagacity, but it enables us
to see clearly some guiding lines in the comparative study of miracles ; for in two significant respects the supposed centaur bears no
analogy to the miracles of the Gospels.

For (1) the centaur is itself a monstrosity. *The centaur*
The miracles of the New Testament are all *a monstros-*
on the plane of nature. Feeding the hungry, *ity,*
healing the sick, raising the dead — all these
are removals of obstructions which hinder nature from being the perfect and direct expression
of God's goodness to man. They are hints of
an ideal state which nature will one day reach,
accelerations of her slower processes. So far
from the truth is Matthew Arnold's dictum
that " from the moment that the comparative
history of all miracles is a conception entertained and a study admitted, the conclusion is
certain that the reign of the Bible miracles is
doomed " — so far is this from the truth that it
is precisely when we bring the miracles of Jesus
into comparison with the prodigies of Greece
and Rome or the grotesqueness of mediæval
miracles, that we more clearly than ever discern
the finger of God and detect, perhaps for the
first time, the essential and distinctive char-

acter of the works of Christ as truly revealing the God of the nature we know.

(2) But secondly and especially, the centaur is an isolated phenomenon; proceeding from nothing, going nowhither, accomplishing noth- ing, signifying nothing, meaningless, irrelevant, incredible. That a man of Huxley's sagacity should compare such an appearance to the Gos- pel miracles is another warning to examine for ourselves; another demonstration that the ablest men may sometimes be satisfied with touching but the surface of a subject. The miracles of the Gospels were wrought by an unique person, by one who has actually revealed God and altered the world's attitude toward God; they were wrought as a part of that reve- lation, and they have actually lodged in men's hearts the conviction that God is merciful and kind. They appear as the natural outcome and concomitant of a manifestation which had been prepared for, and even expected, through a long previous history. Between miracles so imbedded in the supernatural, so congruous to the circumstances, and trailing such a history behind them, and a centaur trotting down Regent Street, where is the analogy?

But it is precisely here where all arguments against the credibility of the Christian miracles fall short. The strongest evidence in their favor is their congruity with the person who wrought them, and with the revelation in connection with which they were wrought; and this evidence is generally, one may almost say regularly, left out of account. In this respect Matthew Arnold, who compares them with the portents and prodigies of Grecian history, is as superficial as Huxley. Of course we should find it difficult to believe in the resurrection of Nero or of Trajan; but, given a person *already miraculous* in his sinlessness, on whose resurrection the hope of the world depended, and I find the incredibility immeasurably diminished. Is it nothing in favor of the miracles of our Lord, that they were wrought for the accomplishment of the greatest end that could be served in this world? Does it make them no more credible, that they were relevant, significant, congruous, necessary? The miracles are Christ's miracles, and that makes precisely all the difference.

In prosecuting the comparative study of miracles we must not, then, be content with recognizing that supposed miracles abound, and that no more credence can be given to those ascribed to Jesus than to those ascribed to Becket or the Bab. We must consider the

Congruity of miracles with Christ's person.

Differentia of Christ's miracles.

differences, as well as the likenesses, which the
various miracles betray, and especially we must
estimate their likelihood by a consideration of
the occasion, the nature, and the worker of the
miracles alleged. Doing so, we find that the
miracles ascribed to Jesus stand on quite a
different footing from those ascribed to other
founders.

Are miracles useless even though proved?

The other objection to the acceptance of the
Gospel miracles which one meets everywhere
at present is, that even if provable they are
useless. The doctrine proves the miracle,
rather than the miracle the doctrine. Thus,
Dr. Rashdall says, " It is not *a priori* inconceivable that in the whole course of history
there should be one single exception to such
a uniform mode of action; but it may well be
thought morally inconceivable that any spiritually important consequences should be depend-
ent on the belief in an historical event which
would be so utterly incapable of establishment
by testimony as a supposed solitary exception
to an otherwise uniform course of nature."

Matthew Arnold's objection.

To this objection Matthew Arnold has given
the classical expression in his well-known
words: " One may say, indeed, Suppose I
could change the pen with which I write this
into a penwiper; I should not thus make what

I write any the truer or more convincing. That may be so in reality, but the mass of mankind feel differently. In the judgment of the mass of mankind, could I visibly and undeniably change the pen with which I write this into a penwiper, not only would this which I write acquire a claim to be held perfectly true and convincing, but I should even be entitled to affirm, and to be believed in affirming, propositions the most palpably at war with common fact and experience." [1]

Every friend of Arnold must wish his pen had been changed into a penwiper [2] before he wrote this sentence, for it shows that he misconceived both the nature and the purpose of the New Testament miracles. It is a libel on the common sense of the mass of mankind to assert that they would be influenced by a mere piece of legerdemain, which had no relation to the truths to be enounced. We accept the miracles of Christ because they embody the very thing to be proved. Miracles are not gratuitous, superfluous, inconvenient, and irrelevant credentials; they are themselves didactic and revealing. They were not cre-

This a misunderstanding.

---

[1] "Literature and Dogma," p. 132.
[2] I seem to have seen this somewhere else; but where, I cannot tell.

dentials of the kind that can be examined, approved, and then laid aside that the substance of the mission may be gone into. They were something very different from the seal on a letter which, as soon as recognized, is torn off and thrown away that the contents of the letter may be read. They were rather like the very contents of the letter, which in every line reveal and certify the writer. They were like the munificent gift which suggests but one possible giver, the far-reaching benefaction which guarantees its own authorship.

Christ Himself the greatest miracle.

But while we believe that our Lord healed the sick, had power over nature, and rose from the dead, the greatest miracle of all was inseparable from His own person: the perfect manhood, the ideal relation to God and man He constantly manifested. It was this, and no external miracle, which drew to Him His earliest and most devoted followers. For, seeing Christ, it was God men saw, and saw Him to be more and better than they had thought.

To escape from the supernatural at this point by denying the sinlessness of Jesus is a sorry shift. This is the crowning, or root miracle which lends credibility to all others: a miracle unique and separating Him from all other men ; a miracle which convinces us that at this point, at all events, He had transcended all human experience and passed into a region beyond human calculation. Is a miracle in the spiritual world less or is it greater than a miracle in the physical? Which is the more divine, the turning water into wine or the perfection of character that is impervious to sinful thought and desire? The one thing is as unexampled as the other, as truly beyond experience.

It is the personality of Christ which enables some to dispense with the miracles He wrought; yes, but it is His personality, also, which makes them credible.